Vikram Seth's
A Suitable Boy

CONTINUUM CONTEMPORARIES

Also available in this series

Forthcoming in this series:

· VIKRAM SETH'S

A Suitable Boy

A READER'S GUIDE

ANGELA ATKINS

CONTINUUM | NEW YORK | LONDON

2002

The Continuum International Publishing Group Inc
370 Lexington Avenue, New York, NY 10017

The Continuum International Publishing Group Ltd
The Tower Building, 11 York Road, London SE1 7NX

www.continuumbooks.com

Printed in the United States of America

Library of Congress Cataloging-in-Publication Data

Atkins, Angela.
    Vikram Seth's "A suitable boy" : a reader's guide / by Angela Atkins.
      p. cm.—(Continuum contemporaries)
    Includes bibliographical references (p.) and index.
    ISBN 0-8264-5707-X (pbk. : alk. paper)
    1. Seth, Vikram, 1952– Suitable boy. 2. India—In literature. I.
Title. II. Series.
    PR9499.3.S38 S8335 2002
    823'.914—dc21
                                2002000880
ISBN 0-8264-5707-X

Contents

My thanks go to Dr. Ira Sarma and Dr. Rupert Snell for their advice on drafts of this book. I am also grateful to the Publicity Department of Orion for giving me access to their archive of reviews.

1

The Novelist

Vikram Seth's family played an important part in the creation of A *Suitable Boy*. Vikram lived with them during the eight years it took to write and edit the book and although he did a lot of research for the novel, much of the information, especially about the shoe industry and the judicial system, came from his parents. Moreover, elements of his characters are clearly recognizable in the biographies of some members of his family. His father, Premnath (Prem) Seth, was an executive of Bata, a Czech-owned shoe company. Seth's mother, Leila, trained in law in London and subsequently became the first female High Court Judge in India.

Vikram was born in 1952, the year in which the second half of the novel is set. In 1954, Prem's job took the family to England for three years and it was then that Seth's mother passed her bar exam, placing first in the whole of England. Seth has a younger brother, Shantum, and a sister Aradhana, a filmmaker, who married an Austrian diplomat. The ways in which these people resemble the characters of Haresh, Savita, and Kakoli do not need to be pointed out. Of his family's direct influence on his writing Seth has said,

My father was not a very literary person, but my mother used to write poetry when she was young. There were always lots of books lying around, so I suppose I was partly inspired by her. Nevertheless, despite my father's lack of interest in the arts, it was he who encouraged me to write (*Garavi Gujurat*).

Seth's grandmother, on whom Mrs. Rupa Mehra is partly modeled, was also a great reader of poetry.

The family moved back to India in 1957 and lived for seven years in Patna, capital of the state of Bihar. Seth has said that Brahmpur is an amalgam of several cities, including Patna. The others are Lucknow, Varanasi (Benares), Agra (all in the state of Uttar Pradesh), and Delhi, which is a state in its own right. All three form part of the "Hindi-belt," so called because Hindi is the main language. However, at Doon School, which Seth attended from 1961–1967, Hindi is only taught as a second language: English is the first language. Situated in Dehra Dun and modeled on an English public school (its first headmaster taught at Eton), Doon is India's most prestigious school. Seth, it seems, has "divided feelings about the place: appreciation for the superb education he [. . .] received and lingering bitterness toward his classmates" (Woodward), a bitterness which came from having being bullied there. On leaving Doon, Seth went to Tonbridge School in England for a year before going up to Corpus Christi, Oxford to read English. However, he soon changed to Philosophy, Politics, and Economics, partly because his father was a businessman and Seth "wanted to be able to see things from his point of view" (*Garavi Gujurat*). Seth also credits the study of economics with helping him to view things pragmatically (*Garavi Gujurat*). Interestingly, Seth has said that he actually found it easier to write because he did not study English literature, perhaps because he was not made overly aware of all those literary giants, to whom he has been compared, looking over his shoulder.

In 1975, after a year back in India, he went to Stanford University, California for postgraduate studies in economics. He has said that it was in Stanford that he learned to have fun (Dougary). Given the humor that runs through his work, it is odd to think of him as a rather serious person before this. While researching his PhD, Seth spent two years at Nanjing University in China and in 1981, during the holidays, he hitchhiked back to Delhi through Tibet before returning to China for another year. The notes he wrote then were to be the basis of *From Heaven Lake*. Back in California, Seth never finished his PhD. He worked instead as an editor for Stanford University Press for two years and wrote poetry, studying for a while with the American poet, Timothy Steele. Known as a polymath (his nickname at Doon was 'genius'), Seth's learning is impressive. He speaks not just English and Hindi but Chinese and German, and, having lived in Calcutta, he is also familiar with Bengali. His linguistic knowledge includes four scripts: Roman, Devanagari (Hindi), the modified Perso-Arabic script (Urdu), and the Chinese characters. In addition to his linguistic knowledge, he is a trained classical Indian singer as well as being an aficionado of Western classical music. Seth has a reputation for being a private person, "hermit-like" as he says, but he puts a lot of this down to the years when he was writing *A Suitable Boy* (Woodward).

The most striking thing about Seth's oeuvre is its variety, as fellow novelist Amit Chauduri wrote.

His career has been one of ceaseless reinvention; from economist to poet, to travel writer, to novelist-in-verse, to popular literary novelist, to librettist, to who knows what next. Skipping from genre to genre, it's as if he's not just a writer, but a microcosm of the cultural ethos. (Chaudhuri, 508)

As if that were not enough, Chaudhuri has not mentioned Seth's incarnation as a translator (*Three Chinese Poets*), and a teller of folk stories (*Beastly Tales from Here and There*). It is not only the genres but also the settings of his works that are disparate. These range from India and China to England and the United States. Such diversity makes tracing the evolution (thematic or stylistic) of Seth's output difficult and less relevant than it would be to a more homogeneous oeuvre. Nevertheless, there are certain threads which run through his work, starting with his collections of poetry.

Even after the publication of two prose novels, Seth declared "I saw/see myself primarily as a poet" (*Guardian* Talk). His first volume of poetry, *Mappings*, was written while he was a student in London and California. Having no luck with publishers, Seth produced his own stapled volume which he hawked around the bookshops of San Francisco Bay in 1980 (*Mappings*, ix). It was not until his trip home to Delhi, during the break from his research in China, that he met Professor P. Lal of the Calcutta Writers' Workshop who published *Mappings* in 1981. The volume includes the intimate subject matter of love, lost love, sexuality, and relationships within the family, as well as poems about nature; he also touches on public issues such as the injustice of poverty. The poem "Dubious" which starts with the stanza

> *Some men like Jack*
> *and some like Jill;*
> *I'm glad I like*
> *them both; but still*

has lead people to make assumptions about Seth's sexuality. It is a question often touched upon in interviews and one Seth refuses to answer. On one occasion he said:

My attitude about the question of my own sexuality is that if people don't like my books then they shouldn't be interested, and if they like my books then it's a pretty poor recompense for the enjoyment I've given them, to try to remove the privacy from my life. (Dougary)

In the same interview, Seth related the depiction of homosexual relationships in *The Golden Gate* not to his own sexuality but to the milieu he was writing about. "It would have been as ludicrous not to include gay relationships in a book like *The Golden Gate* as it would have been not to include religon in a book about India" (Dougary). All of Seth's novels feature a homosexual relationship, but sexual orientation forms only part of a wider discussion about the place of sex in society and in the lives of individuals.

Mappings introduces us to Seth the polyglot with poems translated from Hindi, Urdu, German, and Chinese. The verse is in rhyming couplets, triplets, octets, and sonnets. Seth sees this formal conservatism as the reason he could not at first find a publisher for *Mappings*: "I stood outside the orbit of the latest critical theories, and did not realize that writing in rhyme and metre would make me a sort of literary untouchable" (*Mappings*, ix). So, from his first work, Seth placed himself outside literary trends and attracted the label of "old-fashioned," which was to be used often and, usually, approvingly of *A Suitable Boy*.

The Humble Administrator's Garden was published in 1985. This is a less confessional volume than *Mappings*, though the themes of lost love and the family are still present. It is split into three parts: the first named after the Chinese wutong tree, the second the Indian neem, and the third the live-oak. This continues Seth's interest in the natural world, which enters a *A Suitable Boy* through Mrs. Mahesh Kapoor's well-tended garden. Here too are some portraits: two boys in China who laugh at Seth, a Chinese musician who plays for him, and a depiction of Seth's family at home. As before, the poems are rhymed and in regular meter and verse forms. On the book jacket is praise from fellow poet Donald Davie:

"Vikram Seth's poems should have an impact far beyond much noisier pieces; for when did we last see a volume in which the poet's eye is on what is objectively before him, rather than on the intricacies of his own sensibility?"

All You Who Sleep Tonight, published in 1990 and dedicated to Seth's brother and sister, is similarly outward looking. While the first section "Romantic Residue" explores past love and friendship, another group of poems, under the heading "In Other Voices" depicts historical events: Hiroshima, Auschwitz, and the disintegration of the Moghul empire after 1857. *A Suitable Boy* was to be praised in words which echo Davie's; "[w]hile writers all about him look within, Vikram Seth insists upon looking without" (Yardley).

From Heaven Lake: Travels through Sinkiang and Tibet contains some vivid portraits of the characters Seth met while traveling through China and Tibet, as well as an appreciative description of the landscape. En route, Seth mused on the political administration and its differences to the Indian system of government. He also talked to one Tibetan family about the injustice faced by some in Tibet. Seth values the experience of having lived in three continents and wrote of China,

to learn about another great culture is to enrich one's life, to understand one's own country better, to feel more at home in the world, and indirectly to add to that reservoir of individual goodwill that may, generations from now, temper the cynical use of national power. (*From Heaven Lake*, 178)

A meticulous evocation of setting characterizes Seth's work. The editor of *A Suitable Boy* rather infamously asked Seth where Brahmpur was, so strong is the sense of place attached to that fictional city. This skill stood Seth in good stead while writing a travel book and he received the Thomas Cook Travel Book Award in 1983.

In 1986, *The Golden Gate* was published. This novel in verse about twenty-somethings in San Francisco met with huge acclaim. It uses the verse form of Charles Johnston's translation of Pushkin's *Eugene Onegin* (which Seth praises in the introduction to *Three Chinese Poets*). Each stanza is fourteen lines long with the rhyming scheme ababccddeffegg. Sonnets also have fourteen lines, though different types of sonnets have different rhyming schemes, but there has been some disagreement as to whether the stanzas of *The Golden Gate* are sonnets or not. The lines are octosyllabic and the rhymes are alternately feminine and masculine. A feminine rhyme is one where two or more syllables rhyme, as in "various" and "precarious," and a masculine rhyme is one where the last syllable only rhymes, as with "verse" and "purse." In stanza 5.3, the poet refers to his use of the rhyme scheme of *Eugene Onegin* as "this whole passé extravaganza" but this old-fashioned novel in verse went down very well with the public.

Seth says of *The Golden Gate* that it acted as "a sort of stepping stone" to fiction, being both poetry and fiction (*Guardian* Talk). It is organized in the same way as *Eugene Onegin*: both are divided into chapters and stanzas, with each stanza being numbered 1.1, 1.2, and so on to 13.51. This is a structure Seth was to use in his two subsequent novels. There is little elaboration within stanzas or chapters, instead a world is created through their interplay. In common with *A Suitable Boy*, Seth's novel in verse has "sudden variations of pace and switchback lurches of tone from hilarious to serious to sentimental" (Davis). Like the later novel, it is also the tale of a place as much as of a group of people, so much so that Gore Vidal called it "the Great Californian novel" (Seth, Advanced Publicity). As with *A Suitable Boy*, much of the sense of place is created through language. There is American slang (the "doodads of suburbia" (5.27)—for UK readers "doodad" is American English for thingummy); the technical vocabulary of poetry ("Hudibrastic"

(5.4) that is, in the manner of *Hudibras*, a mock-heroic satirical poem by Samuel Butler); and chess ("fianchetto" (5.14) which refers to moving a bishop one square to a long diagonal of the board). There is also a mistrust of passion which runs all the way through Seth's oeuvre. As one reviewer says it is "not that the novel is without passion — it is bursting with it, but each time passion appears it is, as one of the characters remarks, "a prelude to disaster" (Davis). These aspersions are cast by Phil, whose passionate relationships, first with Claire and then Ed, turned sour, and who marries in the end not for love but for companionship and a family.

After *The Golden Gate*, Seth returned to India to live with his parents in Delhi in order to write *A Suitable Boy*. It was to take six years to write and almost another two to cut. During that time *Three Chinese Poets: Translations of Poems By Wang Wei, Li Bai and Du Fu* came out. The three poets were almost direct contemporaries and lived during the Tang dynasty. Seth writes in the introduction to the volume that his aim as a translator was to be as faithful as possible to the originals, rather than use them as "trampolines" to bounce his poems off. What he has to say about the limitations of translation is interesting given that in *A Suitable Boy* he represents, in English, conversations that have taken place in Hindu, Urdu, and Bengali.

Even in prose the associations of a word or an image in one language do not slip readily into another. The loss is still greater in poetry, where each word or image carries a heavier charge of association, and where the exigencies of form leave less scope for choice and manoeuver. (*Three Chinese Poets*, xxv)

Seth, however, thinks the attempt worth it if he can give "access to the worlds of these poems" (*ibid*). The translations are evidence not only of his skill as a poet but also his abilities as a linguist and a translator. The three poets, as Seth writes in his introduction, are quite different. Wang Wei retreats into nature, Li Bai is full of "the intoxication of poetry or music or wine" while Du Fu reflects, often sadly, "on society, history, the state and his own disturbed times" (*Three Chinese Poets*, xvi). Writers are of course notorious for writing about themselves while puporting to write about others and these concerns are in evidence in Seth's own poetry. What is of additional interest is Seth's liberalism and the even-handedness which permeates all his work, and *A Suitable Boy* in particular. He appreciates all three poets equally although their approaches to life are so different from each other, if not mutually exclusive.

One day, when Seth found it too hot to work on *A Suitable Boy*, he started on *Beastly Tales From Here and There*. The ten animal fables are told, or retold, in rhyming couplets. Two are Seth originals and the others are from India, Greece, China, and the Ukraine. By and large, the tales are evidence of the law of the jungle — the good guy does not win, though in "The Monkey and the Crocodile," the intended victim outwits the aggressor. Aesop's fable, "The Hare and the Tortoise," is given a very modern twist. The hare plays to the assembled media and becomes a celebrity despite losing the race, while the tortoise fades into obscurity. "The Elephant and the Tragopan," written by Seth, features all the animals in a forest banding together to plead with the local human community not to flood their valley.

Before finishing *A Suitable Boy*, Seth took time out to write a libretto for the English National Opera. This was *Arion and the Dolphin*, which was first performed, with music by Alex Roth, in June 1994 with an enormous cast of 450. Arion is a singer in the court of Periander in Corinth who travels to Sicily for a music competition. His prize is a heap of gold, but the sailors on the ship carrying him back to Corinth steal the treasure and throw Arion overboard. He is rescued by a dolphin who takes him back to

Corinth, but Periander does not believe Arion's story and imprisons him. The dolphin is made to do tricks and pines away but Periander, witnessing Arion's genuine grief for the dolphin, sets the musician free and decrees the sailors be put to death. Arion pleads for clemency and the libretto ends with Arion singing the couplet "Warm earth, teach us to nourish, not destroy/The souls that give us joy." Orion later published the story as a children's book with illustrations by Jane Ray. It was also made into a 25 minute animation which was shown in Australia, Canada, and the UK.

Since then Seth has written one more novel, *An Equal Music* (1999). It is set in contemporary London in the world of classical music. Daniel Johnson called it "the finest novel ever written about music in English" and Maggie Gee wrote "Seth gives the fullest portrait I have ever read in fiction of a musician's relationship to his music." Unlike Seth's other two works of fiction this one is told in the first person, through the words of Michael, a 37-year-old violinist who lives in London. He describes the claustrophobic social world of his string quartet; their rehearsals, performances, and the psychology of their relationships with each other. He also tells of his renewed love affair with Julia, a pianist he had been involved with ten years previously when they were both studying music in Vienna. Julia has since married and had a son but she and Michael start an affair that brings as much pain as pleasure to both of them. As in *The Golden Gate* there is still consolation to be found outside oneself: in friendship and the natural world. In this novel there is, in addition, music, which transfigures those who play it and which "is a sufficient gift" (381). A recording was made of the pieces mentioned in *An Equal Music* — a rare example of a CD accompanying a book.

INFLUENCES

A Suitable Boy has been compared to the great eighteenth and nineteenth century European novels of Jane Austen, George Eliot, and Tolstoy. Comparisons between these and Seth's novel tend to hinge on the panoramic depiction of a society. There are some interesting parallels with *Middlemarch*. Published as a serial in 1871–1872, George Eliot's novel is set forty years earlier. There is almost exactly the same time lapse between the setting and publication of *A Suitable Boy*. There are general elections in both novels and two sentences from Rosemary Ashton's introduction to *Middlemarch* could apply almost equally to Seth's novel.

It is above all about change and the way individuals and groups adapt to, or resist, change. In their marriages, in their professions, in their family life and their social intercourse, the characters of the novel are shown responding in their various ways to events both public and private (*Middlemarch*, ix).

The structure of both narratives is similar. They take up the story of one group of people and then after a while lose sight of them, while switching to another group of characters, bringing them all together at the end. However, Anita Desai in the *New York Review of Books* refutes the parallels with nineteenth century novelists: "Seth's touch is feather-light and airy; one can ascribe to it neither the great dark weight of Tolstoy's searching meditations nor the flashing satiric swordplay of Jane Austen's pen." Nor, in her view, does Seth share the "great Victorian zeal for reform that inspired so much of Dickens's and Eliot's work." James Wood in the *Guardian* also contrasts the seriousness of Tolstoy's characters who ask "How may I live better?" with Seth's who according to Wood, "ask cheerfully, 'What's next?'" Some critics are put off by the populist feel of his novels.

The poet, Dom Moraes, called *The Golden Gate* "a Mills & Boon novel" on first reading it (Chaudhuri, 508). Seth admits to having read romance novels but these claims should perhaps be taken with a pinch of salt. When warned to expect questions about his favorite author at the Edinburgh Festival, Seth turned to the critic he was with and asked "Do you have the name of a bad Scottish saga-writer?" On being supplied with a name, Seth vowed that, if asked, he would say he read the novels of Dorothy Dunnett "with the greatest admiration" (Wood). Seth has made a more serious contribution to the debate about popular subjects in his novels, saying, "[l]ove, death, passion, honour, ambition etc. are now treated as the province of so-called airport novels; and that is nonsense" (Rediff. com).

When asked about his place in modern Indian English fiction Seth said: "I see myself as part of a movement in terms of simultaneity of event but not necessarily of common causation [. . . .] But I'm sure that every particle of gas in Brownian motion sees itself as an independent entity" (Woodward). Seth is an open admirer of R.K. Narayan whom he described as "a wonderful writer, the greatest of us all" (Rediff.com). He has also said that he might never have dared to write about North India had Narayan done so. Seth has stated that he avoided reading other Indian English novelists while writing *A Suitable Boy*, in case he was tempted to fill in gaps, or to avoid subjects already covered by them, but he made an exception for R.K. Narayan (Seth, 2001).

Unlike *A Suitable Boy*, Narayan's novels are short, but read back to back, they provide a panorama of small town life in South India. The tales of Malgudi, the name given to Narayan's fictional town, do have an everyday quality that is also found in parts of *A Suitable Boy*, and they too are humorous. However, Narayan uses myth where Seth does not and Seth's characters are more sympathetic. Pico Iyer groups Narayan, Seth, and Rohinton Mistry together in one strand of Indian English fiction which he terms "compassionate realism." He opposes to this the strand of "pinwheeling invention" to which he claims Rushdie, Shashi Tharoor, and I. Allen Sealy belong. Seth's place in Indian English fiction, it seems, is constantly defined by the contrast he provides to Rushdie. Whereas Rushdie's *Midnight's Children* uses the fantastic in the tradition of magic realism, Seth is realistic; while Rushdie draws attention to his language, Seth's prose is clear and easy, and, as Pico Iyer wrote, "Seth is a peacemaker where Rushdie is a belligerent." The comparison was traded on by the publishers of both novelists when *An Equal Music* and Rushdie's *The Ground Beneath Her Feet* came out at the same time and went "head to head." Too much can be made of this contrast however: there are some angry passages in *A Suitable Boy* and Seth too loves to play and show off with language. Moreover, both writers include a depiction of politics in their works and a portrayal of the integral part Indian Muslim culture plays in India.

In his introduction to *The Golden Gate* in *The Picador Book of Modern Indian Literature*, Amit Chaudhuri writes:

Lacking a clearly defined tradition to fall back on, the Indian writer in English, working in isolation, has laid claim, like Borges's Argentinian writer, to all of Western and European tradition, besides his own, in a way that perhaps no European can; and so has Seth, taking whatever, and whenever, he chooses. (508)

There are certainly stylistic elements of *A Suitable Boy* which arise from its Indian setting and the tradition of Indian literature. Devices of popular fiction, as well as a legacy from the great European novels of the eighteenth and nineteenth century are also present. It is Seth's eclecticism which perhaps most defines his writing and it is this which will be investigated further in the next section.

2

The Novel

INTRODUCTION

A *Suitable Boy* is the story of Lata Mehra and her search for a husband. The novel opens with the wedding of Lata's elder sister, Savita, to Pran Kapoor and Mrs. Rupa Mehra's edict to Lata, "[y]ou too will marry a boy I choose." Soon afterwards, Lata falls in love with a dashing young student at her university, whose name is Kabir. Lata is Hindu, and Kabir is a name used by both Hindus and Muslims. However, it turns out that Kabir is Muslim. Lata's mother discovers the liaison and bans it because she cannot bear her daughter to marry a Muslim. She whisks Lata off to Calcutta and institutes a search for a more suitable boy, which turns up Haresh. He is a Hindu of the right (Khatri) caste who works in the shoe industry. In Calcutta, Lata meets the famous poet, Amit Chatterjee, who is her brother's wife's brother, and he becomes the third suitor.

The plot is, in part, driven by the puzzle as to whom Lata will marry. Will her mother's anti-Muslim prejudice be overcome and Kabir be deemed suitable in the end, or will Lata defy her mother in order to marry him? Alternatively, will she accept one of the other suitors? Many of the main concerns of the novel are present in Lata's story: the relationship between the Hindu and Muslim communities, the importance of caste, love and marriage, and the family. These concerns are echoed and developed in the lives of four families around whom the narrative is organized. Three of them, the Mehras, Chatterjis, and Kapoors, are related by marriage. The fourth family, the Khans, are friends of the Kapoors, large landowners and also, unlike the other three, Muslim. The stories of these families bring in other issues: of the value of work, the process of change, the injustice of poverty, and the direction taken by the newly independent and democratic India. The novel is not only a love story but also a depiction of India; however, it does not attempt, as some Indian novels in English have done, to represent the whole of that vast nation. It portrays only a specific slice of it, the middle and upper classes of North Indian society in the early 1950s. Its depiction is, broadly speaking, comic: the tone varies but is most often light, and the plot finishes with a wedding, which is traditionally a happy ending. The tale is an every day one—not Rushdie's magical India full of miraculous coincidences, snake-charmers and soothsayers—but rather a workaday nation of legal systems and industry. *A Suitable Boy* does not always do quite what is expected of it—Lata's choice of husband is the most obvious example. This is because for Seth, "writing is partly a matter of creating genres" (Chaudhuri, 508), and what we have here is not simply a love-story, nor an epic, nor a realist historical novel, neither is it an English novel pure and simple, but rather an Indian novel in English. It is in the synthesis of all these elements that the distinctiveness of *A Suitable Boy* lies.

Because there are so many different editions of the novel, and because the chapters are short, the references given are not page numbers alone but also refer to the chapter number. For example, in the first reference below (1.5:15), 1 refers to the part of the novel, 5 to the chapter and 15 to the page number (of the 1993 hardback edition).

LOVE AND MARRIAGE

Lata's choice, then, is India's choice. The options for each involve either a transcendence of religious factionalism (Kabir), a sophisticated internationalism (Amit, the poet celebrated in England), or a homespun and plodding pursuit of economic stability (Haresh). However, [. . .] Seth is able to convey the subtlety and complexity of such choices without turning his characters into overt symbols. (Filkin, 1993)

The moment in which all three suitors meet at a cricket match (India vs. England) is the one where the symbolism of Lata's choice is most apparent. Of course, what is good for society (Haresh's hard work and economic innovation) is not necessarily good for the individual, and Lata's choice of Haresh is not good for her—is it? There probably is no single answer to that question, and certainly no right one, but it is Lata's balancing act between her own desires and her place in society which is at the heart of the novel.

We begin at the beginning with Mrs. Rupa Mehra, and Savita's arranged marriage. It is Lata who provides the commentary on her elder sister's marriage, and she does so in a way that provides a point of entry for the non-Indian reader to whom the idea of an arranged marriage may be completely foreign. Lata, thinking of the fact that Savita and Pran have only met for an hour previously, is "irritated and confused" by the look of "special tenderness" that Savita gives Pran when he coughs (1.5:15). As for the wedding night, it "did not bear thinking about" (1.9: 22). Lata's attitude, we are lead to believe, is partly the result of a generational shift. Much later in the book, when Amit is being advised to marry by Biswas Babu, Amit says "nowadays people say that you should choose your own life-partner, Biswas Babu. Certainly, poets like myself do" (7.18:418). And yet, Lata by the end of the novel, has agreed to a marry a man found by her mother, albeit someone whom she has met several times and whom she claims to love. How does this transformation occur and is the reader carried along by it?

It is only in the penultimate part that Lata finally rejects Kabir and so the reader is left guessing for 18 of the novel's 19 parts whether she will marry him. In Western love stories there are two typical courses for a love which faces opposition from the family to run. In the first, the hostility of the family to the match remains implacable and tragedy ensues, as in *Romeo and Juliet*. In the second, true love overcomes all obstacles, the family is reconciled to the marriage, the lovers are united, and it all ends happily ever after, as in Jane Austen's *Persuasion*. In terms of *A Suitable Boy*, either Lata can defy everyone, marry Kabir, and live estranged from her family, or Mrs. Mehra can be persuaded to change her view of her daughter marrying a Muslim. The story teases us with the possibility that Lata and Kabir might get married in the end. There are, after all, other love-marriages in this book, chiefly that of Lata's elder brother Arun and the glittering Meenakshi. (Despite the fact that Meenakshi is having an affair with Arun's best friend, she and Arun seem to get along well enough). However, the two cases are not similar, Arun can get away with more because he is a man, and, in any case, Meenakshi, though Bengali and of a different (Brahmin) caste than Arun, is at least Hindu. Kabir tells Lata that he knows of two marriages where one spouse is Hindu and the other Muslim but Lata does not take comfort from this. In the end, Lata and Kabir do not marry and yet the ending is certainly not tragic.

It is possible that the reader is reconciled to Lata's decision because it is realistic. He or she may feel that nothing else was possible in 1950s India. One Indian critic certainly sees it in those terms and thinks, furthermore, that it would have been impossible in 1990s' India to portray a mixed marriage: "in the aftermath of the horrible Indian partition and the resultant communal frenzy, in 1951–1952 it was unthinkable, on the part of Seth, to show an inter-religious marriage" (Agarwalla, 28). But why does Lata reject Kabir? Malati accuses her of giving him up because he is a Muslim and asks Lata to take into account "the danger caused to the world by that sort of attitude" (18.21:1296). Lata does not deny that her decision is partly due to Kabir's religion but the reader is not lead to believe that she shares her mother's prejudice. So is she doing "just what Mummy says" (18.21:1295) as Malati accuses her?

Meenakshi Mukherjee has commented that the conflict between individual desire and family duty is a pan-Indian concern and individual desire is given less importance in India than it is in the West:

Sometimes the conflict resolves itself neatly into two issues: duty to the family, and personal fulfilment. The fulfilment of oneself, however, desirable a goal according to the individualistic ideals of western society, has always been alien to Indian tradition, especially when it is achieved at the cost of duty to the family. [. . . .] Sexual love and personal happiness, those two prime concerns of the Western novelist, do not have such central importance in the Indian context. (Mukherjee 1971, 29)

These are concerns that will be investigated further in the section on characterization but it is important that the reader does not think that Lata has just given in to her mother. If it is felt that Lata has no option but to marry the man her mother chooses, Lata's character becomes less important than the determining conditions of society. The novel then becomes a tragedy.

At first, the influence of Lata's family on her seems to be governed by prejudice and sexism. Mrs. Mehra's dislike of Muslims is ugly and explicit. Lata's position as a daughter means that she has little power to resist decisions made on her behalf. When Kabir asks her to wait a couple of years before they marry she responds "I'll be married off in two years [. . .] You're not a girl. You don't understand" (3.20:186). When Kabir cites the two "mixed marriages" he knows of she replies "[o]urs wouldn't work. No one else will let it work" (18.16:1287). "No one else" in this case is her mother, her grandfather, and even her mother's "samdhin" or co-mother-in-law, Mrs. Tandon. Kabir certainly blames Lata's confusion on her family. Reflecting on the situation, he feels that "he had to try and understand her. The pressure of the family, the extended family that enforced a slow and strong acceptance on its members, was something that with his own father and mother he had never had to face" (13.22:907).

At this point in the novel most readers are keen for Lata to resist that pressure, and yet by the end of *A Suitable Boy*, our view of the situation is more complex. This is because Lata has a greater appreciation of her family. It is partly the birth of Pran and Savita's daughter that changes Lata's perspective. All four families in the novel are brought together by Uma's birth. Lata and Mrs. Mehra take care of Savita, Imitiaz looks after Pran, Mr. and Mrs. Mahesh Kapoor visit their granddaughter, Maan his niece, and even Kuku Chatterji arrives to see her sister's husband's sister's baby. For Lata, "with life and death so near each other here in the hospital, it seemed [. . .] that all that provided continuity in the world or protection from it was the family." Her "mother appeared to her now as the guardian of the family" (13.12:877).

Lata has also developed a different view of the realities of marriage. "Lata had begun to look at marriage (the Sahgals, the Chatterjis, Arun and Meenakshi, Mr. and Mrs. Mahesh Kapoor, Pran and Savita) with more than a disinterested eye" (13.12:877). Mr. Sahgal is abusing his daughter. The Chatterjis have a companionable marriage which is based around concern for their children. Arun claims his marriage is based on trust but he is being deceived, while Mrs. Mahesh Kapoor is the ideal Hindu wife, or a too long-suffering woman, depending on our view of her. Pran and Savita make a very touching couple, they "loved each other—or, rather, had come to do so. They both assumed, without ever needing to state it—or perhaps without even thinking explicitly about it—that marriage and children were a great good" (13.12:876). Lata has recognized at an earlier point that love does not necessarily rest on the choice of one individual for another individual. She realizes that Savita, who loves Pran, would probably have fallen in love with any good man.

But whether it was owing to the hectoring of her mother or her overly copious love or the vision of these different families or Pran's illness or the birth of Savita's baby or all of them combined, Lata felt she had changed. The sleeping Savita was perhaps a more powerful advisor that the voluble Malati. (13.12:877)

As Lata's sister has changed in status and become a mother, so Lata's view of herself has altered.

Lata looked back on her wish to elope with Kabir with a kind of amaze-ment, even as she could not shake off her feelings for him. But where would these feelings lead? A gradual, stable attraction such as Savita's for Pran—was this not the best thing for her, and for the family, and for any children that she might have? (13.12:877)

Lata has begun to think of herself not only as a student of English literature, friend of Malati, and youngest of four children, but as a possible wife and future mother. This changes her view of the sort of man she wants to marry. Malati finds Kabir's letter to Lata "teenage" (12.4:772) and though Lata points out that volunteering to help after the Pul Mela disaster was not the action of a teenager, she too is unsatisfied with his letter. The character of Kabir, in comparison to Haresh, remains sketchy: he studies, plays cricket, and acts well. He also goes to see his mentally ill mother and this, as well as the help he gives at the Pul Mela, speaks of an admirable sense of duty. However, he still seems very young, the ambitions he speaks of to Lata are those of a single man, not one ready to settle down and have a family. In comparison, Haresh has many more connections with the rest of society — with Kedernath and Bhaskar, the Jatav community, Kalpana Gaur, and his own large family in Delhi.

Arun's letter, in which he tries to persuade Lata not to marry Haresh, has the predictable effect of making Lata and the reader like Haresh more. Most of Arun's reasons are based on social snobbery. When Arun talks about his own marriage as "a happy one based on mutual affection and trust" (18.20:1292), the reader of course knows (although Lata does not) that Meenakshi is unfaithful. Haresh, both by his erstwhile constancy to the unobtainable Simran, and his openness to Lata and her mother about his previous love, has shown himself to be trustworthy. The steadiness of his affection for Lata and his positive outlook also recommend him as Lata says to Malati "Haresh is practical, he's forceful, he isn't cynical. He gets things done and he helps people without making a fuss about it" (18.21:1297).

The dangers of marriage without passion are depicted through the character of Rasheed, who made a promise to his dying mother to marry his elder brother's widow. Rasheed does not love his illiterate, village wife and instead becomes infatuated with Saeeda Bai's sister, Tasneem an infatuation which contributes to his descent into madness. Lata tells Malati, much to the latter's surprise, that she does love Haresh, and she can cite the qualities in him that she admires, but she makes a distinction between this love and her turbulent feelings for Kabir. A significant part of Lata's decision rests on her rejection of passion. Citing the devastation that Maan's infatuation for Saeeda Bai has caused to "the family", and linking this to her own jealousy when she thought Kabir was seeing someone else, Lata declares, "what I remember feeling was enough to make me hate passion. Passionately and forever" (18.21:1296). Her rejection of intense desire also has to do with what she has seen of the uglier side of sex, including Mr. Sahgal's abusive relationship with his daughter, Kirin. Dreaming of Kabir one night, Lata is horrified when his face turns into that of Mr. Sahgal. Fear of the strength of her own sexual desire is expressed in an extreme form in this dream but it is evidently something that preys on Lata's mind. She complains "I'm not myself when I'm with him. I ask myself who is this—this jealous, obsessed woman who can't get a man out of her head" (18.21:1296). She later tells Malati that she will not feel she is making a fool of herself with Haresh with regard to sex, whereas she would with Kabir. At their wedding Lata involuntarily holds Haresh's hand more tightly when Mr. Sahgal comes to congratulate the couple. Though Haresh does not know the reason for this, he nevertheless provides Lata with a sense of protection.

Lata's rejection of Kabir is partly a repudiation of the exclusivity of sexual passion. It would not only have made her forsake her family but also her studies. When Lata suggests eloping, Kabir replies he has to finish studying, and at the time this jars. Later on, however, when Malati asks Lata if Haresh will let her teach, she replies that he will. The sort of affection Lata feels for Haresh is not to the exclusion of all else, rather, Haresh offers her the sort of love "which helps you to grow where you were already growing" (18.21: 1299).

Although it might seem obvious that Lata's choice of marriage partner is closely tied to the novel's Indian setting, it is a decision echoed by characters in Seth's other works. In *The Golden Gate*, Phil eventually marries Liz. Both are recovering from passionate relationships which have turned sour. When Phil proposes to Liz, she objects that it would not be wise for them to marry because they do not love each other. Phil replies in words that pre-figure Lata's rejection of passion

> [. . .] *I've found*
> *That love's a pretty poor forecaster*
> *I loved a woman—and was dropped.*
> *I love a man—that too flopped.*
> *Passion's a prelude to disaster.*
> *It's something else that makes me sure.*
> *Our bond can last five decades more.*
> (11.20:244)

Liz agrees, "I too don't feel sure/I can trust passion any more" (11.21: 245). The prognosis for the marriage looks good, at least in the short term because at the end of the novel, Liz, who marries Phil partly in order to have a family, is pregnant. In *An Equal Music* the pianist Julia makes a similar decision. She stays with her husband and child and separates from her lover, rejecting a passion that leaves her too emotional to cope. In a letter to Michael after the affair has ended she writes "I have to learn peace again, for my own sake [. . .] I have become restless with you, and uncertain, and afraid, and guilty, and unsustainably, stupidly full of joy and pain" (324). The man she decides upon is one of Seth's solid types: he "isn't volatile—like me. He isn't moody—like me. He doesn't ask questions that come out of nowhere. He comforted me. He made me happy. He kept me sane. He gave me courage" (327–8). Like Lata, Julia claims to love the man in favour of whom she has rejected a more passionate affair.

There are two poems in *The Humble Administrator's Garden* which reflect on the nature of passion. "A Little Distance" is a poem to a woman who appears to have previously been a lover but is now just a friend. In it the poet celebrates their new-found "uncomplicated" chasteness and admits "Unsettledness/Is what I have come to fear" (21). In "From the Babur-Nama: Memoirs of Babur, First Moghul Emperor of India" love is once more portrayed as a sort of madness. The emperor, who has been in love with a boy, reflects "During my passion I was deranged, nor knew that/ Such is the state of one who is in love"(36). He charges himself with "neglecting the respect/And attention due both to myself and to others"(36). This concern with the effect of love on a wide circle of people, not just on the lover and the loved-one, is typical of Seth. One reader asked Seth why passion always goes wrong in his books. Seth replied that he didn't believe passion always goes wrong and added that in different circumstances, with different people it might succeed (Rediff.com). However, Seth has yet to write the work in which it does.

Returning to Lata and her decision, we see that not only has she formed her own opinion of the place of passion in her life, and the importance of her family, she has also won a certain concession to her individuality from her mother. Whereas Pran and Savita had only seen each other for an hour before they married, Lata meets Haresh on several occasions and corresponds with him before making up her mind. Lata has not extinguished her ego, to use Meenakshi Mukherjee's phrase above. Her marriage to Haresh reflects not outright capitulation but a compromise between her wishes and those of her mother. The reader's acceptance of this compromise is in conflict with the power of the romantic story as a genre—the belief that true love conquers all, and that love is the most valuable of all experiences, for which it is worth sacrificing everything else. When Lata first meets and falls in love with Kabir, the narrative is firmly in the genre of romantic comedy. Lata's decision, however, as we have seen, is formed after her experience of the more fundamental occasions of life: the birth of Savita's baby, Mrs. Mahesh Kapoor's death, and the exposure of the Nawab Sahib's youthful crime. These are moments from outside the genre of romantic comedy and Lata's decision cannot be understood without these. Seth has stretched the genre and spliced it with epic and tragedy in order to represent the complexity of the choice his heroine has to make. How the reader responds to the ending and the issue of who Lata should have married, depends, more than in most novels, on the values the reader brings to the book in the first place. That the novel does not direct all readers to the same conclusion might be seen as a failure of the unity that is required of a work of art. Alternatively, it may be that Seth's democratic liberalism extends to his readers as well as his characters.

HINDU-MUSLIM RELATIONS

When asked what his greatest fear was, Seth replied "that India will succumb to communal hatred" (Greenstreet). Elsewhere he described *A Suitable Boy* as "partly a plea for tolerance" (Robinson). At Partition in 1947, when the land mass that had been British India was divided into India and Pakistan, the largest migration in history occurred as Hindus moved to the truncated India, and Muslims to the country that became Pakistan. There were horrific tales of "trains steaming across the plains with their dead and refugee columns stretching for dozens of miles" (Khilnani). Since Partition, violence has flared up again from time to time. Even after the huge exchange of populations, and although Hindus are far and away in the majority, India still has a sizeable Muslim minority. Nehru, Prime Minister at the time the novel is set, believed that religion had no part in the affairs of state and that moreover, Muslims were as integral to Indian society as Hindus. However, there were others in the Congress party who wanted India to be primarily a Hindu nation, and these two positions are played out in Brahmpur through the characters of Kapoor and Agarwal. Other Indian novels, such as Kushwant Singh's *Train to Pakistan*, and Bapsi Sidhwa's *Ice-Candy Man* depict the horror of Partition but in *A Suitable Boy* it occurs before the novel begins. It is only alluded to through one of the more minor set of characters: Mrs. Tandon, Kedernath, and Veena, who were living in Lahore at the time of Partition and had to escape to India. Although Partition itself occurs offstage, the novel opens only four years after those horrors and they partly form the background to the plot which drives the novel: Lata and Kabir's love.

The affair is declared hopeless almost before it has begun. The first kiss is in 3.14 and only four chapters later Mrs. Rupa Mehra has banned the match. The scene begins comically, with Mrs. Mehra crying so much in the tonga that she gets through her reserve handkerchief, but the tone changes and the depiction of her opposition to the romance pulls no punches; "Never, never, absolutely not—dirty, violent, cruel, lecherous—" (3.18:182). In the very next scene her intolerance is put into a wider context: "Mrs. Rupa Mehra was not more prejudiced against Muslims than most upper-caste women of her age and background" (3.19:182) indeed, as Lata points out to her mother, Mrs. Mehra has Muslim friends. It is not until part 18 that Lata finally rejects Kabir and up until then, there is the hope that Mrs. Mehra might eventually come around. During this time the novel has depicted not only the mutual hostility which threatens civil harmony in India, but also the friendships and shared culture which unites Hindus and Muslims. Within each community there is also shown to be a range of beliefs, and attitudes to belief, which renders it far from homogeneous.

Seth portrays the all too real possibility of communal violence. The Raja of Marh plans to build a temple next to the city's main mosque in order to house a lingam, or sacred phallus, that, it is claimed, once stood in a temple on the same spot. The lingam is now at the bottom of the river but if the Raja succeeds in raising it, the Muslims in the mosque next door will find that when they turn to face Mecca in the West they will be bowing to the lingam. This plot has a resonance with the real incident that occurred in Ayodhya in 1992. Ayodhya is actually referred to by name in the novel, when the Nawab Sahib is trying to persuade Mahesh Kapoor to stand in Salimpur-cum-Baitar (14.17:997). For Hindus, Ayodhya is the birth-place of Ram, avatar of Vishnu, legendary king of a golden era and hero of the epic *Ramayana*. Since the sixteenth century, a mosque has stood on this site. From time to time the dispute over the site flared up and it did so in 1949–1951, the period of the novel. In the 1980s, the right wing Hindu party, the BJP, began to raise the temperature once again with a campaign to pull the mosque down and build a temple in its place. The mosque was in fact demolished with pickaxes and shovels in December 1992 in an episode that sent shockwaves across India and led to communal rioting and deaths. When Seth was asked about his prescience in describing an incident very similar to the Ayodhya affair he answered,

It was a most unhappy prefiguration of events. The mosque and the temple theme was not so big when I wrote it a few years ago. That it should have come to this was unimaginable [. . . .] Many, many Hindus are shocked and ashamed. (Woodward)

In the novel, the outcome of the Raja of Marh's plans to build a temple is very different from the reality of Ayodhya. The lingam proves too heavy to be hauled up out of the river by rope, and rolls back, crushing some of the men who had been hauling it on the way down. Although gravity eventually foils the Raja's plans, tension between the two communities has been raised in the meantime.

These tensions come to a head during the fifteenth part of the novel. The Shia Muslim community is commemorating Moharram and mourning the martyrdom of Imam Hussain at the hands of Sunni Muslims in A.D. 680. The Hindus are celebrating the victorious return of Ram to his kingdom with a *Ram Lila* — a play of the events. Moharram culminates in the procession of *tazias* which are replicas of the Imam's tomb. In the novel, two routes are plotted for the processions which should keep them apart. The evening starts off quietly. Saeeda Bai, as is her tradition, is serving refreshing drinks to the Shia faithful. Maan, using the occasion to get near her, incurs her displeasure for doing so. Bhaskar is part of the Hindu festivities, playing one of the monkey warriors who helped Ram defeat his enemy. Had everything gone according to plan, the night would have passed without incident. Instead, the timing goes wrong and the two processions cross paths. In a virtuoso passage the narrative switches from the point of view of the Muslims, to the Hindus, and back. From the Hindu perspective we see "this lunatic mourning that made a mockery of the enactment of Shri Ramachandra ji returning to his home" (15.11:1057) and from the Muslim side we see "kafirs, leaping about like apes on the very eve of the great martyrdom" (15.11:1057). The chapter ends with the death of three Muslim drummers who had been hired for the Moharram procession but who were not Shias. They lie "murdered by the wall of the temple, their drums smashed in, their heads half hacked off, their bodies doused in kerosene and set alight — all, doubtless, to the greater glory of God" (15.11:1058). For all Seth's reputation as a moderate, this is a sentence of biting irony which would not seem out of place in a Rushdie novel.

The shock of the incident is increased because the evening

started with the trivial romantic concerns of Maan and Saeeda Bai, and the childish excitement of Bhaskar. Characters the reader is familiar with are involved on each side of the religious divide. Although the riot may ultimately be sparked off by the accident of the two processions crossing, it is not seen as inevitable. The Raja of Marh is partly responsible, as is the mullah of the mosque who has been making inflammatory speeches. So, too, in her own small way, is Mrs. Rupa Mehra. Abdus Saleem, referring to the whipping up of religious prejudice during the election says to Mahesh Kapoor,

If only bad people were prejudiced, that would not have such a strong effect. Most people would not wish to imitate them — and so, such prejudices would not have much effect — except in exceptional times. It is the prejudices of good people that are so dangerous (18.15:1284).

Mrs. Mehra does not overcome her prejudice, Lata and Kabir do not marry. However, Maan and Firoz, even after killings of the Muslim drummers and the riot which follows, remain friends and so bridge the divide between the two religions. As Pico Iyer wrote "a Hindu crosses religious lines to befriend a Muslim, and later stabs him — for reasons that have nothing to do with their religions." Their friendship, and the reconciliation of their fathers, is a small triumph.

Two other strands of the story have a direct bearing on the depiction of Muslims in the novel. The first of these is the world of music, the second is land reform.

The social contract that kept Hindus and Muslims in a state of tolerance, friendship and love, nurtured over the centuries by a common interest in the finer things of life, music, dance, and art, is beginning to break up after Partition. An already populist government attempts to bring in legislation which will deprive landholders of their properties, which in turn would mean that all those who were dependent in a feudal system would suddenly find themselves left high and dry, especially musicians and courtesans. (Krishnan)

There are two representations of musical culture in *A Suitable Boy*, and in both, Hindus and Muslims are shown to enjoy the same music. The form of that music is drawn from both cultures. Saeeda Bai is first invited to sing at the house of Mahesh Kapoor on the occasion of the Hindu festival of Holi.

She began her recital with a few Holi songs. Saeeda Bai Firozabadi was Muslim, but sang these happy descriptions of young Krishna playing Holi with the milkmaids of his foster-father's village with such charm and energy that one would have had to be convinced that she saw the scene before her own eyes. (2.4:81)

She goes on to sing ghazals by Mir and Ghalib, two famous Urdu poets who lived in Lucknow. Ustaad Majeed Khan is a much more austere musician. Also a Muslim, he thoroughly disapproves of the use to which Saeeda Bai puts her art. However, like her he sings music dedicated to Hindu gods and he is not even conscious of the fact. Both musicians are affected by Mahesh Kapoor's land reform measures. The Zamindari Abolition Act will lessen the wealth of the patrons who sponsored them, as Saeeda Bai points out to Maan. (Today, the world of courtesans has all but disappeared, its demise hastened by the absence of patronage from the erstwhile zamindars. There are rumors that courtesan culture still exist in cities such as Lucknow, but it is certainly no longer part of the fabric of the city as represented in *A Suitable Boy*.) Majeed Khan is also threatened with loss of income, as he complains to Veena. The Nawab Sahib mentions the Ustad by name when he is telling Mahesh Kapoor of the cuts he will have to make after the zamindari system has been abolished.

The people of Baitar expect me to put on a proper show for our festivals, especially for Muharram [. . .] I have certain other expenses—the hospital and so on, the monuments, the stables, the musicians like Ustad Majeed Khan who expect to be retained by me a couple of times a year, poets who depend on me, various endowments, pensions; God—and my munshi—knows what else. (14.17:996–7)

However, unlike Saeeda Bai, Majeed Khan makes the transition from a world of private patronage to state-sponsored broadcasting by performing for All India Radio. The Zamindari Abolition Act affected Muslim landlords disproportionately because many Muslim families, like the Nawab Sahib's, had already been divided, and so weakened, by Partition.

THE WORLD'S LARGEST DEMOCRACY

A Suitable Boy is partly a hymn to democratic India. Seth had originally intended to write a "series of short novels" covering the period from the 1950s to the 1990s (Woodward) but the action of *A Suitable Boy* starts at the beginning of 1951 and finishes at the end of April 1952. So, why did Seth get stuck in this period? 1952, as well as being the year of Seth's birth, is the year of India's first election by universal suffrage. Elections had been held under the British but the body to whom the British transferred power at Independence had been voted for by a limited electorate. The 1952 election, as the narrator comments, "was in fact to be the largest election ever held anywhere on earth. It would involve a sixth of its people" (15.22:1085). India is the world's largest democracy, as

journalists love to point out whenever India has a general election.
This is a fact that Seth also finds remarkable and in *From Heaven
Lake* he compares the political systems of China and India and
concludes that although democracy is a difficult institution for a
poor country to preserve India has achieved it.

> For all the corruption and abuse that the Indian political system displays, it
> is, after a fashion, both representative (unpopular governments have twice
> been thrown out) and widely accepted (again, it seems to be the norm for
> those born after Independence). This is quite remarkable. (105)

The election that takes place in *A Suitable Boy* is not a shining
example of the democratic process. The seat of Salimpur-cum-
Baitar, which Mahesh Kapoor contests, is won by someone with no
political experience or principles who exploits religious prejudice.
Waris Khan, a servant of the Nawab who had been put up as a
dummy candidate in case Mahesh Kapoor did not get nominated,
wins the election. However, this is only after he has distributed a
flier announcing the death of Firoz at Maan's hands and claiming
the murderer is free on bail "to strangle more helpless Muslim
women and slaughter the flower of Muslim manhood" (17.35:
1244). Kapoor is urged to file a complaint but refuses. Back in
Brahmpur there is a comical but damning depiction of the importance of political influence even in areas which should be free of it,
such as academia. Professor Mishra does not want to appoint Pran
as reader but feels he has to endorse his candidature when he
believes Pran's father has been re-elected. It is only after he has
given Pran the job that Mishra discovers that Mahesh Kapoor has
in fact lost the election.

Democracy, however, is not purely about elections but rather
functions through a variety of institutions in addition to parliament.

In *From Heaven Lake*, Seth writes of some of the other components of a democracy including, "a court with independent powers to interpret a functioning constitution" and "a press that can criticise the executive" (106). The depiction of the passage of the Zamindari Abolition Bill through the courts, although largely comic, shows a judicial process entirely independent of any political influence. The press does not play a prominent role in the novel, but when it does appear, it is characterized precisely by its divergence of views and its cricitcism of the authorities. After the Pul Mela disaster, one newspaper blames the police for what went wrong, another the administration, a third the slippery condition of the ground, and so on, until an "eighth blamed the national character" (11.27:750). The narrator, typically, makes fun of such an abstract notion as "national character" but he also makes a more serious point "Wherever the truth lay, if anywhere, everyone insisted on an Inquiry" (11.27:750). It is precisely because the truth is so hard to determine, and because there are such differing views in society, that a free and active press is needed.

The concern with democracy is not limited to a depiction of the mechanics of a democratic state — something that might be termed the spirit of democracy infuses the novel. Just as different, and even conflicting, interests find a voice within a democratic society, so this novel is partly remarkable for the even-handedness with which it treats mutually exclusive positions. This is nowhere more in evidence than in the land reform narrative. As David Myers wrote, Vikram Seth

is capable of seeing both sides of the issue simultaneously. The need for land reform to give a chance to the destitute serfs of India was of course morally obvious. Nevertheless, the Zamindari bill will mean the curtailment of the more benevolent forms of feudalistic patronage. (96)

We have already encountered the effect of reduced patronage on the courts and courtesans of Brahmpur; the reader's sympathies are also engaged for the downtrodden peasant, Kachheru. Under the British, much of northern India had been subject to the zamindari system, whereby zamindars collected rent for themselves and revenue for the government. The zamindar's status gave them enormous power. If a tenant farmer did not pay up, the zamindar could have him evicted from the land which would lead to the destitution of him and his family. This is exactly what the Nawab Sahib's munshi threatens to do to one poor tenant, until Maan intervenes by grabbing the munshi by the throat. In addition to paying rent, tenants were often forced to work for free, and the narrative represents these historical conditions.

It was expected of Kachheru that whenever there was rain during the dry summer months he would go for the next day or two into his master's fields and plough them while there was still water in the soil [. . . .] It was exhausting labour, and it was not paid for. (8.10:531)

It is mostly in the sections in Debaria that the lower castes enter the novel. Part of Seth's rumination on the workings of democracy in *From Heaven Lake* is the thought that the very poor and helpless are not necessarily served well by it.

I remember reading a question in an economics textbook: "If you were to be born tomorrow, would you prefer to be born in China or India?" If I could be guaranteed the lucky place in the Indian sweepstakes that I at present occupy, there is no question as to what my answer would be; even if I were poorer than the average Chinese child, I would still prefer to be in India. But if I were born to the inhuman, dehumanising misery in which the poorest third of our people live, to the squalor and despair and debility that is their life, my answer would not be the same. (Seth, 1983:104–105)

The Zamindari Abolition Act was one attempt to raise the standard of living of one sector of the rural Indian poor. It was passed in order to try and lessen the zamindar's power, by taking away the right to collect revenue. Laws which ensured that any farmer who had been tilling the same field for more than a certain number of years could not be turned off it were also strengthened. After challenges in the courts, which are depicted in Part 11, the Act was passed. However, it failed to make a difference to the peasant in the short term, for various reasons. These include a lack of will in the local Congress Party, represented in the novel by the venial Jha, to enforce the rules. In addition, loopholes in the law were exploited by landlords.

Even today, the majority of the population of India is involved in agriculture and yet Seth is one of the only Indian novelists in English to depict rural areas. Raja Rao, one of the giants of Indian fiction in English, set his 1937 novel, *Kanthapura*, in a village. Rohinton Mistry's *A Fine Balance* begins in one, but in general, the Indian novel in English is an urban affair. In his depiction of agrarian relations, Seth takes up a theme which connects him to some of the more famous Hindi novelists. Phanishwarnath Renu wrote a novel in which the failure of the Zamindari Abolition Act is depicted, and Premchand, often called the father of the Hindi novel, also sets much of his fiction in the villages of northern India. As has been noted, Seth has not tried to represent the whole of India in his novel, but by representing the rural world he has widened the scope of the modern Indian English novel.

It was suggested earlier that one of the things *A Suitable Boy* has in common with *Middlemarch* is a concern with the process of change. Mahesh Kapoor's Act is an example of an active attempt to bring about progress in society, through the mechanisms of state. A much smaller improvement is brought about by Haresh, this time through individual example. By dint of hard work and perseverance he obtains a management position in a shoe company run by Europeans. At the Praha factory he increases production by showing the workers in his charge that he can make as many pairs of shoes in a day as he is asking them to. Beforehand, Haresh secures a promise from the management that if production goes up the workers will not be laid off and he assures his staff that he will press for them to go up a pay grade and resign if they do not. His reasoning during his campaign is worth noting:

Haresh had learnt about the elaborate, sanctified hierarchy of Praha—it was worse than the Civil Service: there were eighteen different grades for workmen. But he felt that it could, without unhinging the universe be given a tiny nudge here and there. (16.8:1115)

Haresh promotes change in other ways too. In particular, he is careless of caste boundaries. He invites the low caste leather-worker, Jagat Ram, to his wedding and asks a man who is lower caste, but older than himself, to sit in his presence. Haresh also thoroughly enjoys the work of making shoes even though it involves handling the hides of dead animals, traditionally unclean work done only by outcasts. In all these small ways, Haresh is giving the sanctified hierarchy of the caste system in India a small nudge here and there.

STRUCTURE

When Lord Gowrie wrote that *A Suitable Boy* needed a good edit and Robert Towers that "the narrative as a whole is diffuse" they were complaining about the novel's structure. In a book on narrative called *The Classical Plot*, the expectations that Western readers have of the formal construction of a plot are described. These expectations have been passed down from Ancient Greek and Roman narratives and they lead to a feeling that a story should "stand as an organic whole, a single self-contained causal chain—closed at beginning and end, and bound together internally" (Lowe, 62).

There are internal connections between the different subplots in *A Suitable Boy* but the structure of the novel as a whole is a loose one. The story of Lata and her suitors is tightly plotted. This is partly shown by the occurence of coincidences. It is Kabir who finds Bhaskar at the Pul Mela and Malati who is misinformed about who Kabir was meeting where. These by turns encourage and frustrate the reader's desire for Kabir and Lata's love to triumph. Maan's love for Saeeda Bai and his stabbing of Firoz also conforms to the standard rules of plotting. It is commonplace in the nineteenth century epics to which *A Suitable Boy* is compared, such as *Middlemarch* or *War and Peace*, to alternate several story lines featuring different sets of characters. This not only paints a broader picture of society but creates suspense. Seth's novel does alternate the plots which concern the four families. However, there is a lot of detail in this novel which is peripheral to any of the main plots: land reform, shoemaking, the internal workings of the Congress Party, and so on. Seth was aware of the issue, as the second of the book's balanced epigraphs from Voltaire shows. "The secret of being a bore is to say everything." We know from Seth's poetry that he enjoys working within strict forms, so why did he not do so with *A Suitable Boy*?

The novel has 19 sections, divided into a total of 477 small chapters, which are, on average, less than three pages long. As has been previously mentioned, this structure means that one scene reflects on another, rather than any depth being developed within an individual chapter. Interestingly, the longest parts of the novel, seven and thirteen, (127 and 111 pages respectively) are the ones which depict family life. In this way, the importance of the theme of the family to the novel is reflected in its form.

Amit, talking to Lata and Dr. Ila Chattopadhyay about his novel, compares it to a raag.

First you take one note and explore it for a while, then another to discover its possibilities, then perhaps you get to the dominant, and pause for a bit, and it's only gradually that the phrases begin to form and the tabla joins in with the beat . . . and then the more brilliant improvisations and diversions begin, with the main theme returning from time to time, and finally it all speeds up, and the excitement increases to a climax. (7.9:394)

Dr. Chattopadhyay dismisses the comparison as "utter nonsense." Later Amit describes a banyan tree and his book in terms of the Ganges:

it sprouts, and grows, and spreads, and drops down branches that become trunks or intertwine with other branches. Sometimes branches die. Sometimes the main trunk dies, and the structure is held up by the supporting trunks [. . . .] But then it's also like the Ganges in its upper, middle and lower courses—including its delta—of course. (7.41: 483)

All three similes (raag, banyan and Ganges) imply size and a diffuse, organic structure. All three images are also Indian. Raja Rao, in his famous foreword to *Kanthapura*, described the traditional Indian narrative as rambling.

And our paths are interminable. The *Mahabharata* has 214,778 verses and the *Ramayana* 48,000. [. . . .] Episode follows episode, and when our thoughts stop our breath stops, and we move on to another thought. This was and still is the ordinary style of our story-telling.

The structure of *A Suitable Boy* draws on this tradition to some extent. Anita Desai, in her review, makes a comparison between *A Suitable Boy* and "the Sanskrit epic in which, through all the di-

gressions and diversions, the thread of narrative is maintained." Seth
has adapted the Western novel form to an Indian subject and narrative pattern.

In her book on the Indian novel, *Realism and Reality*, Meenakshi Mukherjee writes that Indian novelists have always adapted the
form of the novel. She argues that the Western novel was predicated
on the idea of the individual which did not exist in the same way
in India. One's marriage partner and, under the strict caste system,
one's occupation, were not matters of personal choice. As a conse-
quence, the relationship between the individual and society was
very different in India than in the European birthplace of the novel
and so Indian novelists transformed the genre. As we have seen,
Lata's selection of a husband is not a matter for her alone and so *A
Suitable Boy* depicts the middle-class, Northern India milieu of the
1950s in which she makes her decision.

A Suitable Boy is not only a portrait of one particular society, it
is a celebration of society in general, that is, of the tendency and
ability of humans to live with others in a complex and highly varied
structure. A different form is needed to represent a whole society
than to depict the story of an individual or a small group of individuals. The method of using parts, subdivided into chapters, was not
only employed by Pushkin, as has already been noted, but also by
the eighteenth century novelist Henry Fielding in *Tom Jones*. This
novel is also arranged into books with chapters: 18 books with
between 7 and 15 short chapters in each and, like *A Suitable Boy*,
it too paints the portrait of a whole society rather than just an
individual.

Fielding's novel does conform to notions of classical plotting, but
this has certain consequences. He manipulates the plot and the
characters in order to fit preconceived ideas about the world. Seth's
method is almost the opposite: certain parts of the novel seem
virtually autonomous from the demands of the main plot—the

worlds of Praha and Debaria, for instance. It is important for Seth's representation of society, and for his plea for mutual tolerance, that the extent of the difference between various sectors of society is not underestimated. The interests of Kachheru are opposed to those of Rasheed's family, and to those of the Nawab Sahib of Baitar. It is in the courts that the Act which will negotiate between those interests is debated. However, the court proves to be yet another discrete world, more concerned with legal minutiae than with anything the reader can relate to Kachheru, Rasheed's family, or the Nawab Sahib. It is the juxtaposition of scenes and characters that argues for the necessity of seeing another's point of view. Although the novel succeeds in creating multiple viewpoints, the semi-detached nature of many of the centers of interest may leave the reader feeling that the competing claims of the different parts of the novel are not resolved satisfactorily in the narrative.

There are unifying factors: the book ends where it begins, with a marriage. The four families also provide a frame through which to view the narrative, as do Lata's three suitors, and the geographical locations of Brahmpur, Calcutta, and Debaria. David Myers has argued that the novel is unified by the theme of the renunciation of passion. Thematically, the need for compromise in a democracy, the virtues of restraint, and the place of Muslims in Indian society all integrate the disparate parts. Variations on a theme also connect different groups of characters. There are parallels, between Lata and Tasneem, both of whom have three suitors. Three different people talk of the effect the Zamindari Abolition Act will have on Muslim culture, as we have seen: the Nawab Sahib to Mahesh Kapoor, Saeeda Bai to Maan, and Majeed Khan to Veena. The emphasis is slightly different each time because of the context but such instances of elaboration on one issue tie the novel together.

One part of the novel which feels semi-detached from the rest is the section set in Calcutta. However, there are threads running through it which connect it to the rest of the book. One of these is play with language — Kakoli's couplets and Amit's poetry. In Calcutta, as elsewhere, there is an awareness that the Muslim community in India has been weakened by Partition. Amit's father realizes that there "was not a single Muslim judge in the Calcutta High Court in 1948" (7.37:471) because they had all emigrated to Pakistan. Finally, of course, the Chatterjis, as one of the novel's four major families, play their part in one of the novel's central themes: family life. They form a group which bears some resemblance to the body politic — their breakfast meeting is compared to a parliament. The clashing of their interests is mostly confined to who has access to the car (or the telephone) for the day. Nevertheless, as in the wider society, some sacrifices to the greater good are required. In this case, it is Dipankar who has to give up meditation in order to earn money. There is an exuberance to these chapters which illustrates the joyful, anarchic aspect of India. Seth, keen to characterize India not as an exotic mystery, but as a nation-state with mundane economic and political systems, does, in this section, give free rein not to exoticism but to an inventive playfulness.

CHARACTERIZATION

Vikram was originally named Amit until his father's family decreed his name should begin with a "V", but Amit is the name on his birth certificate. There are obvious resemblances between Seth and the poet Amit but we should be careful of drawing absolute parallels. Seth has said "[e]ven characters based on real people change when they come into contact with those whom they haven't met in real life" (Guardian Talk). Seth is so fond of his fictional protagonists that the Hindi translation of *A Suitable Boy* is actually dedicated to one of them — Mrs. Mahesh Kapoor. Seth is quoted as saying "I got so involved with the characters and the period I had chosen to begin with that the novel grew broader and deeper." (Seth, Advanced Publicity) He apparently started the novel with a scene between Mrs. Mehra and Lata and then several months later found he "had opened the door partly wide and there were all these people walking into this huge drawing room [. . . .] They were strolling about uncontrollably" (Woodward). Seth talks of them living with him still even after he has finished the book (Seth, Advanced Publicity). When asked why the novel is so long, he says that he could not have cut it without cutting the characters (Tressider). However, if there is one thing on which the critics disagree more than any other, it is Seth's characterization. As far as one camp is concerned, his people are loveable and memorable, but for the other camp they are too sketchily drawn, too shallow, and too static to be really interesting.

The main cause for complaint seems to be that the characters are not drawn in the psychological mode of much modern fiction. In fact, Seth specifically warns against reading the novel in Freudian terms: "anybody who tries to read Oedipal complexes into this novel . . . would be doing the Freudian thing which I am trying to avoid. Freud is a fashion and a fact, but I think he explains very little of the world." (Field) It is possible to infer psychological reasons for the behavior of some of the characters. The strength of Maan's infatuation with Saeeda Bai may, in part, be due to his position as the younger son of an overbearing father, a father whose main priority is his public work, not his private relationships. Maan may well be driven to seek affection in unsuitable places and so turn an idle infatuation into a desperate passion. However, the narrative does not encourage such speculation. The comment in the novel that Maan has "a real sense of warmth" when "his father was far less dismissive of him than usual" (17.5:1167) is in no way connected by the narrator to Maan's passion for Saeeda Bai. The interest in who Lata marries does not come from her psychology. A comparison with Dorothea, the heroine of *Middlemarch*, is instructive. Dorothea's first marriage, to the infirm and cold Casaubon, is very unhappy. Dorothea, like Lata, is restricted in her choice of husband because of the expectations on a woman of her class. However, Dorothea's mistake is directly attributable to her extraordinary mental state, her unrealistic ideals, and the passion with which she pursues them. Lata, on the other hand, is not unique in the dilemma she faces, as the parallels between her situation and Simran's show, nor is her mindset the focus of attention in the narrative. She does not chose Haresh, as she might have done in a "modern" or "Freudian" novel because her father died early, nor does the fact, mentioned to Malati, that she does not think sex with Haresh will embarrass her suggest she has sexual hang-ups. When Lata is asked by Malati how she has come to her decision to marry Haresh, Lata refuses to divulge any psychological reasons and simply replies that she has consulted her monkeys and read some poetry.

A Suitable Boy, it seems, is more interested in the interaction between people in society than in the psychology of the individual. A comparison between two eighteenth century English novelists (Richardson, author of *Clarissa*, and Fielding) throws light on Seth's technique.

Richardson, no doubt, takes us deeper into the inner workings of the human machine; but Fielding is surely entitled to retort that there are many other machines in nature besides the individual consciousness [. . .] he was engaged in the exploration of a vaster and equally intricate mechanism, that of human society as a whole, a literary subject which was, incidentally, much more consonant [. . .] with the classical outlook. (Watt, 301)

We will return to Seth's classical outlook but it is interesting to note that it was typical of the "classical tradition as a whole [. . .] to avoid the intimate and confessional approach to personality" (Watt, 284).

The society which Seth depicts, traditionally places less emphasis on the "inner workings of the human machine" than European society, so that Seth's characterization may be partly mimetic. Mrs. Mahesh Kapoor suffers from a lack of opportunity for direct self-expression in relations with her husband. He, for instance, thwarts her desire for Hindu ceremonies repeatedly. However, small details do create a sense of her individuality: the way she slips domestic questions in among the Assembly reports she reads to her husband is one example of this, and her prize-winning garden, with its unorthodox puddles is another. She also embodies an ideal, recognizable as a type in Indian literature and society, that of the model Hindu wife who, putting the needs of her husband and children before her own, will not eat until after her husband has eaten, does not contradict him openly, but still guides his opinions through a life of unobtrusive virtue. When Veena, Bhaskar, Kedarnath, and Kedernath's mother go to stay at Prem Nivas after Bhaskar's accident "Mrs. Mahesh Kapoor made no mention of any additional strain this arrangement imposed on her" (12.2:766). Her character would have particular resonance with a reader who recognized "the patient heroine" of a tradition whose works of literature often "extol the virtue of the extinction of the ego" (Mukherjee, 1971:29) and who was aware of the debate surrounding the role of women during the nationalist struggle leading up to Independence in 1947, four years before the novel opens.

The humor inherent in the portrayal of many of the characters in *A Suitable Boy* is gained precisely by ensuring that we keep our distance from them and by providing them with one or two traits which never vary. These include Lata's grandfather's alternating fits of anger and weeping, Kakoli's monopoly of the phone, and Meen-akshi's vampish behavior. (Contrast, for example, our view of Meen-akshi's liaison with Billy with the pain-racked affair in *An Equal Music* and it is clear how little we take her, Billy, or Arun seriously.) Though Dr. Seth, Kakoli, and Meenakshi remain wholly comic figures, other characters move between two modes. Mrs. Rupa Mehra too has fixed comic traits: her black handbag, her fondness for sweets, and her sentimentality. Her veneration for her late hus-band is represented by the use of a capital whenever she refers to him (an honor usually reserved for God). When Mrs. Mehra asks "Do you think it is easy for me, trying to organise things for all four of my children without His help?" (1.1:3) "His" refers to her hus-band. The reader becomes so used to Mrs. Mehra's self-pity about her widowhood that it is mostly a comic device. However at one point in the novel, the gap between Mrs Mehra and the reader is closed as she laments that her husband will never hold her again. This momentarily changes our perceptions of her from fussy mother to a woman who has lost the man she loved.

All characters, major and minor, are defined not so much through a description of their consciousness, self-expression, or view of themselves but through their relationships with others and other's view of them. The reader thoroughly applauds Maan's attack on the munshi who is punishing a peasant for not paying the rent. It is only later when Sandeep Lahiri, the local SDO, asks Maan how he knows that there were no repercussions for the peasant that Maan's quick temper appears in a new light. Of course, his anger is to have very serious consequences later in the novel. Maan's passion for Saeeda Bai is also seen from different angles. It is mostly depicted as amusing, endearing, and titillating. However, during the scene in which Saeeda Bai and Tahmina Bai cheer themselves up with imitations of their clients, Saeeda Bai does "quite a good impression of Maan making desperate love" (13.9:866) and this reminds us with a jolt of the commercial nature of their relationship and seems to demean not just Maan but Saeeda Bai as well. Mahesh Kapoor's secularism is much valued by Muslims including the Nawab Sahib, and it is a quality endorsed by the narrative. However, Mahesh Kapoor has his own extremism: at one point he baits his wife that neither of their sons will perform the "shraadh" rites for them when they are dead (14.29:1026). His secularism is unbalanced and he is harder on his co-religionists than on Muslims. However, just because the major characters are defined externally through their relationships with others, rather than through their consciousness, this does not stop the reader relating to them. We do not need to know the inner workings of Lata's mind in order to feel with her in the decision she has to make. We see Lata looking after Varun, looking up to Savita, by turns affectionate towards and angry with her mother, and affected by the calamities suffered by her brother-in-law's family. We understand, without the help of Freud, why she chooses Haresh—because she cannot imagine life without her family. We understand, because we cannot imagine her life without her family either.

The value given to self-expression in the West is something associated with Romanticism. Although it is nineteenth-century novels to which *A Suitable Boy* is usually compared because of its panoramic depiction of society, in one respect all Seth's writing is more akin to the classicist spirit of the eighteenth-century and its emphasis on universal experience and common humanity. Lata's musings on the family which lead her to make her decision are all to do with universal experiences and values, as we have seen. It is the ultimate universal—death—that, as in *The Golden Gate*, acts as a catalyst. Rasheed and Mrs. Kapoor both die during the course of the novel, and Firoz, Pran, Bhaskar, and Maan are also all in death's shadow at some point. Through these experiences Mahesh Kapoor comes to realize the value of his wife and his son, Maan to understand that passion has to be controlled and Saeeda Bai to experience love for Maan. A novel that concerns itself with the intricate mechanism of human society and that balances diversity with common humanity will tend not to concentrate on the idiosyncrasies of psychology. Raymond Williams's comment on Jane Austen is applicable to Seth: "it is not personal relationships, in the abstracted sense of an observed psychological process, that preoccupy Jane Austen. It is, rather, personal conduct: a testing and discovery of the standards which govern human behaviour in certain real situations."

Mahesh Kapoor's conduct is tested when he has to decide whether he should use his influence to try and get the charges against Maan reduced. As a prominent politician, to do so would be immoral; as a father, not to do so would be inhuman. Trying to look at this and other decisions through his deceased wife's eyes Mahesh Kapoor wonders "which of his several duties — or conceptions of duty — she would have expected him to follow" (17.28: 1225). The dilemma Mahesh Kapoor is faced with calls for a reassessment of the balance between his public and private life, something which has, from the perspective of his family, previously been out of kilter.

Woodward states that Seth's "artistic heroes — Mozart, Pushkin, Jane Austen — reflect a nature more in step with enlightenment values than modernist experimentation. Everything Seth has published relies on clarity and wordplay, on passion and anxiety bridled by classical forms". So Maan must learn to control his passion, because passion in the public sphere leads to the sort of religious riots in which Firoz is nearly killed the first time. The values needed in a society threatened by conflict are restraint, tolerance, liberalism, secularism, generosity towards others and a willingness to forgive. The characters themselves act charitably towards each other and the narration treats them warm-heartedly. The rhyme Savita writes in Lata's book advises both compassion and stoicism.

> *Life is merely froth and bubble.*
> *Two things stand like stone:*
> *Kindness in another's trouble,*
> *Courage in our own.*
>   (16.23: 1150)

In this spirit, Firoz forgives Maan and also tries to reconcile himself to his own father's youthful rape of Saeeda Bai. The Nawab Sahib, inspired by Firoz, also forgives Maan, and Firoz claims to have fallen on his own knife, thus getting Maan off charges of attempted murder. Characters are drawn in the acceptance that people have idiosyncrasies and serious flaws — the important thing is not why they have them but how those around them will adapt to accommodate them.

LANGUAGE

Seth said that he wanted his writing "to be like a pane of glass between the reader and the subject, not brilliant stained-glass that simply gets in the way" (Jones). Undoubtedly the straightforward prose, with its short and uncomplex sentences, speeds up the reading process, foregrounds the plot and makes the book, for all its size, an "easy" read. The style cannot be taken for granted, however, not least because the depiction in English of a predominately non-English speaking society raises issues that have concerned many Indian writers. Why write in English at all? Only a small percentage of the Indian population is literate in it. The answer varies from writer to writer of course, but access to a global readership and higher financial rewards are common to all. In Seth's case, although both Hindi and English are spoken in his parental home, his schooling was in English. There probably never was much of a choice for

Seth about the language in which he wrote, because he is part of that sector of Indian society which is most comfortable in English. Amit, when asked during his poetry reading in Brahmpur why he does not write in Bengali, replies "that his Bengali was not good enough for him to be able to express himself in the manner he could in English" (18.2:1253).

The task of an Indian writer in any language is complicated by the multilingualism of Indian society. India has two official languages: Hindi and English, as well as a dozen other major languages and many, many more dialects. The majority of people in India encounter more than one language in their daily lives and to represent the speech of an individual in one language will nearly always involve some degree of translation. English, however, brings its own particular problems. Raja Rao, in the foreword to *Kanthapura*, wrote "One has to convey in a language that is not one's own the spirit that is one's own [. . . .] We cannot write like the English. We should not. We cannot write only as Indians." Rushdie, over 50 years later, in the title essay of *Imaginary Homelands*, takes a similar view to Rao, saying of British Indian writers, "I hope all of us share the view that we can't simply use the language in the way the British did; that it needs remaking for our own purposes" (17). Both Rao and Rushdie created first-person narrators whose idiosyncratic voices — neither British English, nor Indian English, nor translated vernacular — color the narratives.

Seth's approach is rather different: *A Suitable Boy* is narrated in the third person in grammatically standard English, with a peppering of untranslated Hindi, Urdu, and Bengali words. In passages where these vernacular words are absent, the narration does indeed use language "in the way the British" do. Seth says he chose such a narrative style not in order to be "revolutionary or reactionary" but because "[w]ith such a large caste of characters a strong voice would have been too much" (Robinson, 1993b). The narrative passages are less than half the story however, because *A Suitable Boy* is remarkable for having a high proportion of dialogue which incorporates many forms of language. The types of English range from the educated British English of Lata or Amit to the comically mangled idioms of the Chatterji's Babu; the speakers' competency varies from perfect to poor. In addition there are those forms of English which belong to a particular part of society: the idiotic rhyming couplets of the Chatterji family for instance; the language of the courts where "the impugned act contravenes certain specific provisions of the Constitution" (11.2:688); or the specialized vocabulary of St. Sophia's girls school where a "cad" refers not to a badly-behaved man but to a good-looking one (by way of a Cadbury's chocolate bar). The use of the vernacular also varies from nouns which have passed into English such as "sari," through foodstuffs like "paratha" and "samosa"—familiar to a large section of the non-Indian population of the UK and United States, to more obscure words such as "patwari"—the keeper of land records. On occasions there is a complete sentence, slogan, or rhyme in the vernacular, such as the one with which Jagat Ram's daughter entertains Haresh:

Ram Ram Shah	*Ram Ram Shah,*
Alu ka rasa	*Gravy made from spuds,*
Mendaki ki chatni—	*Chutney made from female frog—*
Aa gaya nasha!	*Drink it, and you're drunk.*
	(4.11:223)

Some of the variations in this matrix of language-use follow significant divisions in society; others, such as that of the Chatterji's Babu and the law courts, are mostly for comic effect.

The use of unglossed words is a feature Seth's novel shares with nearly all Indian novels in English and indeed African and Caribbean ones too. Occasionally, the Western reader is left with only the gist of a sentence as when Bhaskar complains that Maan has not been to see the Ramlila, and says, "You must come tonight, or I'll be kutti with you." Maan replies, "You can't be kutti with your uncle" (15.6:1040). (To be kutti with someone is to break off a friendship). Usually, however, it is easy for the reader to guess the meaning, and the flow of the story is not interrupted. Sometimes nouns are glossed directly: Mrs. Mahesh Kapoor "was the samdhin — the 'co-mother-in-law' " of Mrs. Rupa Mehra and Mrs. Tandon (3.17:177). At other times, a juxtaposition of Hindi and English makes the meaning obvious as when Kabir takes Lata on a trip down the river and calls the boatman. " 'Aré, mallah!' The boatman, however, made no attempt to row towards them" (3.13:163). Some words are made clear by repeated use throughout the novel such as the suffix "-wallah" which is used in a similar way to the English "-man": as in tonga-wallah (a man who drives a tonga or horse and cart), Congress-wallah (a member of the Congress Party) and so on. In a similar way the reader soon comes to recognize that anything the diabetic Mrs. Mehra requests is likely to be a sugary food.

In the introduction to *Three Chinese Poets* Seth warns that "Even in prose the associations of a word or an image in one language do not slip readily into another" (xxv). Despite this, the poetry collection contains no untranslated words, so why is the technique so different in *A Suitable Boy*? Novels have always been intricately bound up with the depiction of a certain time and place in a way that poetry has not necessarily. Untranslated words communicate the existence of objects and concepts specific to the society portrayed and different from any named in English.

The novel has been translated into Hindi by Gopal Gandhi. In a review of the translation Harish Trivedi, Professor of English at the University of Delhi, wrote, "Of all the spectacularly successful Indian novels in English of recent years, it is *A Suitable Boy* which is [. . .]

the most intimately complicit in the local language". Seth's English, Trivedi writes, has a "doubleness" which, while being acceptable English, often reflects at the same time the sentence structure and pattern of Hindi. In Seth's preface to the translation, he writes that Hindi resonated in his ears while he was working on many of the dialogues. The extent to which a reader is aware of this "doubleness" will vary enormously depending on how familiar they are with the vernacular. There are approximately five-hundred untranslated words in *A Suitable Boy*. These place the novel in the geographical region of Northern and Eastern India where they are spoken. They tend to cluster around certain areas of culture: religious practices and the caste system; kinship patterns; food and drink; clothes, plants and animals; exclamations, and terms used in North Indian classical music. The non-Indian reader is confronted with unfamiliar words—these signal unfamiliar concepts which need to be grasped in order for the book to be fully understood. For example, terms for relations are much more precise as well as extensive in Hindi than in English. The use of the word "samdhin" conveys the idea that the relationship of co-mother-in-law is one that is recognized in India and that Mrs. Mehra, Mrs. Kapoor and Mrs. Tandon are not meeting just as friends but as relations. The following are some (but not all) of the Hindi words covered by the English word "uncle": *mama*: mother's brother; *mausa*: mother's sister's husband; *phupha*: father's sister's husband; *chacha*: father's younger brother. All are terms used in the novel. Traditionally one's relationship with these different types of "uncle" would be affected not only by their personality but also according to the position they occupied in the joint family. Using the English word "uncle" would obscure this, while giving the precise relationships in English would be very clumsy. The array of Hindi terms, on the other hand, embodies the importance of family in Indian society and in this novel.

The question of how people with divergent interests live together in society has been touched on previously and is one of the major themes of the novel. Language fits with this concern because it is both a means of communication, binding people together, and also a marker of difference. All four of the families at the center of the book operate bilingually, speaking English and one vernacular language, though switching between the two to different degrees.

	Frequently Used	*Less Frequently Used*
Mehras	English	Hindi
Chatterjis	English	Bengali
Kapoors	Hindi	English
Khans	Urdu	English
(Srivastava, 2000)		

Language divides and connects in several different fields. Many of the state boundaries in India are drawn along linguistic lines. Mrs. Mehra is prejudiced against Lata marrying Amit because she does not want all her grandchildren to speak the Bengali language. Arun and Meenakshi, Lata and Amit, on the other hand, completely bypass the difference in their regional languages (Hindi and Bengali are about as close to each other as Spanish and Italian) by speaking in English. There are very few vernacular words in the sections set in Calcutta reflecting the "brown-sahib" mentality of Arun and the cosmopolitanism of the Chatterjis. Although English can overcome regional separation it inscribes class, gender, and educational differences. The only person of the four main families not to speak any English is Mrs. Mahesh Kapoor—it is difficult to imagine a male character of her background being similarly unfamiliar with the language. Netaji, though of a landowning class, has had a rural education and is cut out of the conversation the SDO has with

Maan when the two suddenly switch to English. Haresh, when judged by Arun, is considered an unsuitable marriage partner for Lata partly because of his less than perfect English. On the other hand, people are shown talking to Haresh in Hindi, including Jagat Ram and the machinists at the shoe factory, and this is part of Haresh's characterization as a man of the people, impatient with the class and caste divisions of India and willing to get things changed.

One of the divisions most threatening to the cohesion of Indian society, as we have seen, is the divide between Hindus and Muslims. From the middle of the nineteenth century, Urdu, with its fund of Persian-derived vocabulary, became associated with Muslims, and Hindi, incorporating more and more words from Sanskrit, with Hindus. However the two languages, while being written in different scripts, still share a common syntax and an overlapping core vocabulary. It is only at the more literary or formal ends of each language that the two become mutually unintelligible. For day to day purposes, the two spoken languages are often mixed with each other. Mahesh Kapoor, for example, can read the Urdu script but not the Hindi, and the use of both languages is fluid. However, there are times when the differences between the languages becomes important. This is shown dramatically when Veena phones Baitar house during a riot in order to let the Khan family know that Firoz is safe and staying with her and Kedernath. She uses the phone of an anti-Muslim neighbor. Veena manages to convey the message in neutral language which does not give away Firoz's presence in her house. But then, at the end of the conversation, she says "khuda haafiz"—the Muslim phrase for good-bye. The neighbor eyes Veena strangely but fortunately does not question her. It is sad that languages whose everyday use overlapped could so suddenly become a source of danger.

3

The Novel's Reception

The novel received plenty of attention even before its publication. This was partly due to its length — at nearly 500,000 words it is longer than *War and Peace* and is the longest novel in the English language to be published as a single volume. It was also due to the huge £250,000 advance which Vikram Seth received from Phoenix, an imprint of Orion, his publishers in the UK. At the time, this was the largest ever advance for a first novel. The story of the auction that Seth's agent, Giles Gordon, held in the summer of 1992 to obtain the sum, became part of literary gossip before the book hit the shops. While Gordon played one publisher off against another and the bidders dropped out, one by one, Seth hid in Gordon's garden. In the United States, Harpercollins paid a reported $600,000 advance for the rights, thus bringing the combined U.S. and UK advance to over $1 million. The publicity that Orion sent out with the advance copies of the novel was equally extravagant:

Bold comparisons invite the reviewer's rebuke, but with *A Suitable Boy* they are irresistible: it stands with Thackeray's *Vanity Fair* as an exploration of human foible, with Eliot's *Middlemarch* as a story of courtship, with Tolstoy's *War and Peace* as a commentary on the fate of nations.

The initial print run of 20,000 in the UK was huge for a first novel, especially for a hardback and one which was priced at £20. But by March 19th, six days before publication, 13,000 of those copies had already been ordered by booksellers and the rest were snapped up in the next week, forcing the publishers to order a reprint before the book had even gone on sale. All this excitement affected the buying public and it was reported that *A Suitable Boy* had sold out in some bookshops within minutes of reaching the shelf and, incredibly, that customers were waiting for trucks to deliver more stock. (Howard)

The reviews were glowing. In Britain, James Wood of the *Guardian* called it "rich and epical." In the *Times Literary Supplement*, Pico Iyer declared the work "a modest *tour de force*" while Peter Kemp for the *Sunday Times* concluded that the publisher's comparisons with Tolstoy, Eliot, and Austen "come to look more and more fitting as the book expands." Daniel Johnson of *The Times*, in a phrase that was picked up by American reviewers when the book was published in the United States wrote:

A *Suitable Boy* is not merely one of the longest novels in English: it may also prove to be the most fecund as well as the most prodigious work of the latter half of this century—perhaps even the book to restore the serious reading public's faith in the contemporary novel.

It was not just the serious literary periodicals, such as the *Times Literary Supplement* and the *London Review of Books*, which gave it coverage but also general publications such as *Vogue* and the Australian magazine *HQ*. In America, Anita Desai, writing in the *New York Review of Books*, compared the experience of reading the book to listening to a raag "played by a musician with skill, dexterity, and charm." Peter Filkins, in a special for *USA Today*, called the novel "masterly" and "that rarest of books, a literary tour de force, as pleasant as it is unpretentious." The cover story of one issue of *Time* Magazine, in February 1993, was a feature by Pico Iyer on postcolonial writers, including Seth. The novel was also chosen for the Book-of-the-Month Club (an American mail-order bookclub which sends its subscribers a specially printed edition of it chosen book every month).

The publicity continued right through the summer as *A Suitable Boy* was chosen in innumerable summer reading lists, and even included by the panel that recommends books for the Queen during her annual holiday at Balmoral. The Booker Prize controversy (see below) made *A Suitable Boy* news again in the autumn and then it was time for the book of the year roundups before Christmas. The following year Seth was the subject of an edition of the BBC program *Omnibus*, made with the help of his sister Aradhana, and presented by Nadia Haggar. *A Suitable Boy* went on to win the £10,000 W.H. Smith Literary Award in April 1994 and the Commonwealth Writers Prize for best novel in October of the same year. In 1997, over four years after publication, a Good Book Guide poll declared it one of the 10 best books published in the last 20 years, and in the summer of 2001, eight years after its publication, at least two bookshops on London's Charing Cross Road featured *A Suitable Boy* as a staff choice.

The reviews in India, like those elsewhere, often concentrated on the size of the advance, an alleged 2.7 crore (the attentive reader who has followed Bhaskar's conversations with Haresh carefully will know a crore is ten million, or "ten to the seventh power"). There were also gripes about the cost of a copy and Tabish Kair in *The Sunday Times of India* joked that the "native literati [. . .] has been confronted with another existential dilemma—to buy or not to buy.

If they buy a book worth Rs 500, they might have trouble existing for the rest of the month". Despite the high price, Penguin India were confident enough to order an initial print run of 7,000 copies. Indian reviews also got caught up in a debate which has rumbled on in India for decades about how authentically Indian the Indian English novel really is. Seth himself was nervous about the novel's reception and declared "I hope *A Suitable Boy* will be most appreciated by people in India. If they think I have exoticised India for the sake of foreigners, then the book is a failure no matter how the book sells." (Roy) Sonal Patel, who was present at a reading session in Bombay, thought that Lata's search for a husband was a "tired theme" and added that Muslim-Hindu relations were better depicted in the television series *Tamas* (which was adapted from the Hindi novel of the same name). However, S. Krishnan, in the *Indian Review of Books*, wrote that it "is completely Indian, from beginning to end." He was particularly impressed by the realism of Seth's depiction of society.

The research Seth did for the book was voluminous, patient, time-consuming, and absolutely impeccable. He recreated debates in the legislature and arguments in the court which sound so exactly like the real thing that one gets the illusion that he must have got them out of official reports, which of course he did not (S. Krishnan).

Harish Trivedi, writing on the use of language in *A Suitable Boy* concurred: "we have in Seth's *magnum opus* an awareness and even a celebration of the cultural Indianess of the Indian novel in English, which remains unparalleled."

There were detractors, however. One Australian reviewer, Rob Johnson, raised an issue which did not feature in any of the UK reviews: the many untranslated words used by Seth. Johnson argued that the book would have been improved with the addition of a glossary. Jonathan Yardley, of the *Washington Post*, likewise pointed to the "profusion of Indian names, nouns and religious terms [. . .] at times so confusing as to make *War and Peace* seem by contrast the very model of crystalline clarity." Yardley recommended going with the flow of the story, though later in the review he brought up the issue again, writing that "Seth's determination not to explain a thing to the Western reader leads too often to gratuitous confusion." Richard Woodward, too, asked "will he translate for Americans who, unlike the British, share no East-meets-West colonial history with the subcontinent?" It is unclear whether the contrast with UK reviews was down to the greater familiarity with Hindi and Urdu words of British readers (due not only to Britain's colonial past but also to the make-up of its multicultural present) or whether non-British critics are simply less inhibited about mentioning such things.

While some reviewers quibbled with the publisher's comparison of the novel to the nineteenth century European greats, others complained about Seth's characterization, or the dullness of the sections about land reform and politics. It was the criticism from Lord Gowrie, Chairman of the Booker Prize in 1993, which received the most publicity. *A Suitable Boy* did not even make the shortlist (which consisted of *Paddy Clarke Ha Ha Ha* by Roddy Doyle; *Scar Tissue*, Michael Ignatieff; *Remembering Babylon*, David Malouf; *Crossing the River*, Caryll Philips; *The Stone Diaries*, Carol Shields; and *Under the Frog*, Tibor Fischer). The row that erupted was colorful even by Booker Prize standards. Lord Gowrie justified the omission of the book on the grounds that it was "abysmally edited and tailored [. . .] promising lines of development and tension kept running out. The book needs cutting, like a movie" (Lambert). The Chairman of Orion Publishers, Anthony Cheetham, was moved to call the Booker judges "a bunch of wankers" (Nevin) and a party was thrown to celebrate the success of the book on the evening before the Booker dinner, although the publishers claimed this was a coincidence. The book had been an enormous success, selling 100,000 copies of the hardback by August in the UK alone.

On the issue of structure, Tim McGirk in the *Independent*, agreed with Lord Gowrie. The "novel sprawls. It spreads. It foliates exuberantly. But it doesn't move." Even Pico Iyer, a fan of the book, complained that the "parts are better crafted, and so more satisfying, than the whole." Desai, however, far from finding the book insufficiently edited as Gowrie was to do, wrote "it is precisely by interweaving all their tales with such skill into patterns of such intricacy that Seth achieves his effect of bulk and mass impossible to overlook." David Myers, in one of the few full-length critical studies of the novel, argued that the book had "been wrongly accused of being diffuse and disjoint" and in fact has a "thematic unity" (79). S. Krishnan thought "the strands [. . .] pulled together brilliantly to make a cohesive whole." Patrick Skene Catling of the *Evening Standard* praised Seth's "extraordinary power of grand synthesis" and Trevor Fishlock in the *Sunday Telegraph* was of the opinion that the novel is not "sprawling" but rather "controlled, and as intricate as an Indian tapestry." In the cassette version of the novel, Lord Gowrie was to get his wish for a more edited story because the narrative has been heavily cut to fit the time constraints. In the next section, the effect the cuts have on the narrative will be discussed.

Characterization was another issue which divided the critics. Robert Towers wrote in the *New York Times*,

In his drive towards inclusiveness, [Seth] has sacrificed intensity. He does not stick with any one character long enough—even the most promising or interestingly troubled—or probe deeply enough to achieve the kind of impassioned empathy that renders a character unforgettable.

Tim McGirk complained that even when depicting major characters Seth "flits off and doesn't deepen our understanding or even our interest in them." Richard Jenkyns in the *New Republic* protested that Seth "seems unwilling to hurt his characters, and this is ultimately debilitating to the novel: if you prick his people, they do not bleed [. . . .] They suffer no pain because there is nothing inside them except stuffing," and Myers argued that every "character, no matter how central a figure, is limited to one or two characteristics" (88). Anita Desai did not see any development in the protagonists and added that Seth, unlike Eliot or Dickens, is too "tolerant of his characters to want to transform them." James Wood also thought the comparisons to Tolstoy and Eliot fell down on the matter of characterization because:

Vikram Seth lacks the moral concentration, the intensity and didacticism of these writers. Characters in Tolstoy and Eliot ask "How may I live better?" and suffer the proper agonies of the unanswerable [. . . .] The characters in Seth's novel look at each other and, with an unbreakable faith in each other and the happy consolations of sequence, ask cheerfully, "What's next?"

Yardley on the other hand found the protagonists fully realized.

Each is a wonderful character who, over the long unfolding of the plot, develops in ways that are convincing, appropriate, pleasing and not a little heart-breaking: each of them becomes sturdy and real in the reader's mind, so that letting them go at the novel's end is far from easy.

Pico Iyer picked up on the warmth of Seth's characterization and wrote "Seth clearly loves his people, and he passes that love on to us. He shows them selfish, quarrelsome and idle, yet never without sympathy."

Comparisons with the other bestselling Indian writer in English, Salman Rushdie, were inevitable. Seth was constantly asked in interviews what he thought of the fatwa imposed on Rushdie after *The Satanic Verses*. There was also an incident which both writers claim was misreported but which proved too juicy a piece of gossip not to be repeated until Seth wrote a letter to *The Times* quoshing the rumor. Rushdie, bumping into Seth at a party, is supposed to have said "I hear you are writing a soap opera." Seth, in his letter, maintained that "Rushdie simply said 'I hear you've written a book'. Since it was known that the manuscript was something of a doorstep, he said it with an ironic smile. But his tone was entirely warmhearted." Anita Desai, herself an eminent Indian English writer, remarked that Seth "has little in common" with other Indian writers in the post-Independence generation, continuing "he writes as if Salman Rushdie had never written *Midnight's Children*." Pico Iyer, as we have seen, wrote of two strands of Indian fiction: one by Rushdie and Shashi Tharoor, and the second a strand of "compassionate realism" by Seth, R.K. Narayan, and Rohinton Mistry. James Wood likewise contrasted Rushdie and Seth, this time in their use of English. "Rushdie's brilliance" in *Midnight's Children*, Wood wrote, was to use the way in which Indian English differed from British English as one of the book's "verbal strategies, and to make a new, spirited language of puns and compounds." Seth uses language more conventionally. Again he likened Seth to Mistry and Narayan, in whose work there is "much fun with adverts, brandnames and nicknames."

In the reviews there was a search for what may best be termed the spirit of the book, or its philosophy. Critics picked on different aspects but what is described is a warm and liberal sensibility. Pico Iyer talked of the way in which Seth sees every angle of a question. David Myers too wrote that Seth sees both sides of the issue of land-reform and that Seth writes "in favour of all moderation, tolerance, rationality and self-discipline." (92) For Anita Desai, if the book has a philosophy, it is "Aristotle's golden mean — the avoidance of excess, the advisability of moderation, the wisdom of restraint, temperance, and control." These classical virtues were highlighted by Richard Woodward as we have seen. James Wood was the most eloquent on the subject, writing of Seth displaying in the novel a "great, breathing generosity" and, in the words of George Eliot's description of Goethe, a "large tolerance."

On the subject of Seth's prose style, Woodward argued that everything Seth has published relies on "clarity and wordplay." James Wood applauded the "loose, styleless prose" of *A Suitable Boy* which is "relaxed to the point of conversation" and one Indian critic suggested that "the sheer simplicity of Seth's prose may be put down to the fact that he is an accomplished poet who does not feel the need to prove himself when it comes to using the language" (*Garavi Gujurat*). Not everybody liked Seth's writing style however. Paul Bailey complained that every "known cliché is employed, and re-employed. Adverbs abound, in order to make clear what should be obvious from the dialogue, of which there is far too much."

According to Pico Iyer, it is the ordinariness of Seth's portrait of India which makes the novel stand out. "The distinguishing feature of the novel, though, may simply be its uneventfulness, its surpassing dailiness, the way in which Seth catches a life-sized, human, unextraordinary India". By setting the novel in a year that wasn't "particularly memorable in modern Indian history," Seth "displays his proclivity for the common-place and quotidian" (Desai). Even Lord Gowrie commented approvingly on Seth's inclusion of the world of work (Lambert). The unusually in-depth and detailed portraits of land reform, the shoe industry and the Congress Party, all contribute to the realism of the novel. They also add to the sense of

India as a country which functions much like any other nation state, though with its own peculiarities, and in this way Seth is true to his intention not to exoticize India for a foreign readership.

One significant omission from the reviews is any discussion of Lata's marriage to Haresh. This, presumably, is because the reviewers did not want to give away the ending. However, it is usually the first subject raised by the "common reader." At a reading for *An Equal Music* (Seth, 2000), Seth was asked if Lata had married the right person and he replied that he didn't really know. The person who asked the question said she was not sure either. When asked online why Lata married Haresh and not Kabir, Seth replied "Do you think I decided the matter? Lata decided for herself and I'm not sure I approve of her decision"(Rediff.com). The majority of readers seem not to approve, either.

4

Adaptations

In December 1994, it was announced that Channel 4 were to make a 13-part adaptation of *A Suitable Boy* for television, spearheaded by David Putnam and Verity Lambert. It was going to be filmed on location in India at a cost of £1m an episode. However, two years later the project had been scrapped and in November 1996 the *Daily Telegraph* reported that Peter Ansorge, deputy head of drama at Channel 4, was not satisfied with the final drafts of the scripts. He said that because *A Suitable Boy* was such a huge book "there was a real sense of loss when it was adapted for the screen." Even though the cinematic medium would add much to the novel in terms of visualization and dramatization, the cutting required would mean a net loss. This suggests that the wealth of detail in *A Suitable Boy* is not redundant but integral to the pleasure of the work.

A SUITABLE BOY ON RADIO AND CASSETTE

The book has been abridged twice, once for a cassette version and once for a BBC World Service radio reading, produced by David Hitchinson. The latter was broadcast in 15 episodes of 15 minutes in August 1997, and so tied in with the celebrations for 50 years of Indian Independence on August 15th. It was partially dramatized by Sayeed Jaffrey who is reputedly very proud that he created 87 characters. Both versions were abridged by Neville Teller, an editor of many years' experience, who has done much work for radio. The cassette version condenses the story into approximately 6 hours of listening, that is 8 cassettes of 45 minutes each. It is thoroughly enjoyable but the extent of the cutting involved is astonishing: from approximately 500,000 words, the text has been reduced to 56,000 words: almost 90% of the novel has gone. Neville Teller has said:

My guiding principle was to adhere as closely as my technical constraints permitted to the main line of the main plot, and to use such other aspects of the novel as could be included to deepen the listener's understanding of the context within which the main plot is played out.

The main line of the main plot is, clearly, Lata's search for a husband. The context in which it is played out includes the relationship between the various religious communities in India, concerns about caste, and the position of women after marriage. Only a very limited amount of material that was not directly related to Lata's search for a suitable boy could be included. Listening to the cassette, one would never guess the depth of the cuts, and the novel on tape does stand as a work on its own. However, if compared to the original, there is, as Peter Ansorge said of the film scripts, "a real sense of loss." The biggest cut is to Parts 8 and 10 which are culled in their entirety. These are the sections, set in the village of Debaria, which feature Rasheed, his family and the peasant Kachheru whom they make destitute. The passage of the Zamindari Abolition Act through the courts is also excluded and with the absence of the land reform subplot, the novel loses its depiction of the first big economic and judicial test of the newly independent country. It also no longer has the distinction of being one of only a handful of Indian novels in English to portray rural life. Moreover, with the exception of Jagat Ram whom Haresh visits with Kedernath, the lower castes are not represented in the novel and the social mileu of the story becomes entirely confined to the urban middle-classes.

The cassette version is much more genteel than the original in several ways. The darkest parts of the novel, including Mr. Sahgal's advances to Lata and the abuse Tapan suffers at school, are edited out. Both of these episodes contribute to the general theme of the danger inherent in sexual passion, in which Lata's choice of husband is to be understood. Maan, who like Lata spends the novel under the shadow of an arranged marriage, provides an important foil to her. However, his gradual dissolution, in which his passion for Saeeda Bai is linked to gambling and drunkenness, is not shown and his trip to Debaria is described as a "self-imposed" exile rather than banishment by his father for bad behavior. As a result, the occasion on which he stabs Firoz comes rather out of the blue. The scene in which Maan eventually rejects his feelings for Saeeda Bai is cut although this parallels and seems to endorse Lata's rejection of Kabir.

Another omission which makes the cassette version more tame than the original is the absence of extreme language. There is not much swearing in the book but on occasions it contributes to the depiction of heightened emotions. When Maan and Firoz are faced by a Hindu mob, during the riots which follow the clash of the

Moharram and Ram Lila processions, Maan growls at one of the mob, "[g]o home and lick up your own blood, you sister-fucker, before I break your neck" (15.12:1061). His anger momentarily confuses the crowd and the two are able to escape. However, on tape the expletive (a direct translation of the Hindi) is left out and with it goes some of the force of Maan's fury, which on this one occasion, has an unequivocally positive effect. The ugliness of Mrs. Mehra's prejudice against Muslims, which disturbs our idea of her as a comic figure, is likewise not portrayed. In the book she labels Muslims as "dirty, violent, cruel, lecherous" (3.18:182) and winces at the thought of Lata becoming pregnant by Kabir, but these lines are omitted from the cassette.

The world of the tape is less rational than that of the book. The depiction of how and why events occur is particularly important to Seth's portrayal of religion in India.

Though many pages of *A Suitable Boy* are devoted to religious rites, processions, myths and beliefs, Mr. Seth's own attitude toward these phenomena seems determinedly secular—as if one of his aims is to demystify India, to counteract the Western notion of wonder-working holy men and gurus of profound spirituality. (Towers)

The satirical portrait of gurus at the Pul Mela is omitted. Equally significantly the background to the riot in which Maan saves Firoz is not portrayed on cassette, so that the reader does not know why it started. We are not made aware that it is partly because of a trick of the calendar that two processions, one Hindu and joyful, one Muslim and sorrowful, are occurring on the same day, or that arrangements had been made to keep them separate and that these had gone wrong. We do know that the Raja of Marh has been stirring up communal tension with his plans to build a temples, but the riot is represented not as something with identifiable causes, which could be avoided in future, but as the result of an ever-present sore.

The balance between the three suitors is changed. Amit does not feature a great deal. The listener remains hopeful about Kabir's suit for longer than the reader does because the tape omits an important conversation between Lata and Kabir. This is the one in 13.22 in which Lata describes the pressure she is under from her family and declares that their marriage would not work because nobody would let it work. Lata's extended musing on marriage in 13.12 in which she reassesses the importance of her family to her is also, crucially, cut.

The tape also misses out some of the humor. Gone is the Chatterji's Biswas Babu with his mangled English idioms, so too is the jargon of the courts, the old lawyer Bannerji who argues the case for the zamindars and keeps his mistress in a railway carriage, and "A Hymn to Mother India" which Dr. Makhijani reads to the Brahmpur poetry society in 3.9. One of the features which characterizes all Seth's writing and not just *A Suitable Boy* is the extent to which he mixes different genres and moods. With the absence of many of the comic touches, the cassette version is more unified in tone than the original. In the book, during the tragic narrative about the Pul Mela disaster, there is a comic scene in which the police requisition Dr. Chand Seth's car. The reader is amused to find the cantankerous old man, before whose anger everybody usually cowers, for once bested in an argument. The omission of this episode from the tape changes the tone of the scene: the tension is increased but only at the expense of the breadth of portrayal. In the book there is the perception that whatever extremes of emotion are experienced by one person, or in one place, elsewhere, life goes on regardless. This brings a certain sense of perspective to the most tragic event and contributes to a theme which runs through the novel and indeed all of Seth's work—the need for feelings to be restrained.

Although Seth was not involved in the process of cutting the novel for the cassette, he insisted on being the reader, partly in order to make sure of the pronunciation. This, for the non-Indian reader, is the major gain of the cassette. The devanagari script in which Hindi is written is phonetic and sounds match symbols almost entirely so there is none of the confusion that exists in English between "read" and "read" and "bough" and "cough." The roman script cannot convey the difference between Hindi's long and short vowels, or between the four types of "t" and "d" for example, except with diacritical marks which would look ludicrously academic in a novel and would in any case only help those readers familiar with the system. However, with Seth reading, it becomes clear, for instance, that Lata rhymes with "butter" and this makes sense of Meenakshi's nickname for her — "Luts." Undoubtedly, Seth's lightly-accented, English-educated voice is a constant reminder of the Indian setting of the novel, even in the narrative passages in which there are no untranslated Hindi or Urdu words. It also serves to place most of the characters in that upper-class world to which they, like Seth, belong. Seth reads rather than acts, although there is a hint of Arun's hectoring tone, and Lata and Malati's conversations take place in the upper registers of Seth's voice.

Not surprisingly, the structure of the story is much tighter. The tape ends as it begins, not just with a wedding but with almost the same sentence when Mrs. Mehra instructs Varun "You too will marry a girl I choose." The omission, referred to above, of the whole of Part 8 means that no sooner has Mrs. Mehra said she is going to visit Kalpana Gaur in Delhi at the end of Part 7 than she is at Kalpana's house at the beginning of Part 9. With the omission of the narrative about land reform, much of the detail of Kapoor's tribulations in the Congress Party and Haresh's battle in the shoe factory, the novel becomes a love story rather than a novel of society. It is more intense, it is also more like a popular romantic novel. Some of the distinctiveness of the original has been lost along with the realistic and detailed depiction of society, which many readers revel in.

In March 2002, a new version of *A Suitable Boy* was broadcast on BBC radio. The four-part serial, which is available on cassette, is quite different from the previous recordings because it is a dramatization. Produced by David Dryden, it has a cast of 42, including Ayesha Dharkar and Rahul Bose and was recorded on location in a Maharaja's palace in Pune. It is a tribute to the novel's enduring popularity that, despite the difficulties involved in abridging the novel, a third adaptation has been made in under a decade.

ANTHOLOGIES

A Suitable Boy was included in *The Vintage Book of Indian Fiction*, which was published in 1997 to celebrate the 50th anniversary of Indian Independence. The anthology was edited by Salman Rushdie and he chose sections 3.9 (Dr. Makhijani's patriotic poem), 3.10 (Malati's phone-call telling Lata that Kabir is a Muslim), and 3.18–3.19 (Mrs. Mehra's reaction to the news). These passages relate the central drama of the book—Lata's love for a Muslim and her mother's prejudice. However, they also include a comic episode and so the balance between seriousness and humor is maintained. Rushdie, in his introduction to the anthology, notorious for its trumpeting of Indian fiction in English and its denigration of translated, vernacular Indian fiction, writes of the "naturalistic but lighter, more readily charming prose of Vikram Seth." (xxi) Amit Chaudhuri in his more recent anthology which, unlike Rushdie's, included much Indian fiction in translation, chose sections from *The Golden Gate*. In so doing he ensured that in this anthology Seth is represented as a diasporic poet living at the time, in America, rather than as a novelist of Indian society.

· **5**

Further Reading and Discussion Questions

DISCUSSION QUESTIONS

1. Does Lata marry the right man? At what point in the narrative does the reader lose hope that Lata will be able to marry Kabir? Which events tease the reader with the possibility that they will marry? Are you disappointed that Lata rejects Kabir? Does your view of him change as the novel progresses?

2. Is Haresh attractive? Do you believe that Lata loves him, or do you, like Malati, think she is making a mistake that she will live to regret?

3. Is Amit taken seriously as a suitor by the reader, or does the reader, like Lata, find the thought of him as a husband laughable?

4. Do you feel that a marriage between Lata and Kabir would have been impossible, given the realities of 1950s India? To what extent is Lata's choice based on her own best hope for happiness, on the one hand, and submission to the pressures of

society, on the other? What place is played in her decision by her family?

5. If you, like Lata, examine the other married couples in the novel (Mr. and Mrs. Mahesh Kapoor, Savita and Pran, Arun and Meenakshi, the Sahgals, and the Chatterjis) how might you characterize their marriages? What light, if any, do these relationships shed on Lata's decision?

6. It has been suggested that Kabir, Haresh, and Amit represent different paths for the newly Independent India. To what extent are you encouraged to view them as symbols of Muslim-Hindu unity, the virtues of hard work, and cosmopolitanism, respectively?

7. It has been noted that all three of Seth's novels, and some of his poems, display a distrust of passion and place a high value on restraint and family life. Does the rejection of passion provide a thematic unity to the novel as Myers has suggested? What implications does the novel's attitude towards extreme emotion have for your view of Lata's decision to marry Haresh?

8. Do you find the characters likeable and plausible, or two-dimensional and without sufficient psychological depth? Do they develop, or rather remain unchanged throughout the story? Is there any evidence, for example, that either Mahesh Kapoor or Maan learns from his experience? If self-revelation does not play an important part in Seth' characterization, how are the characters created? How might the novel's depiction of the workings of a society have affected its characterization?

9. What do you think of the darker scenes in the book — Mr. Sahgal's abuse of Kirin, the bullying of Tapan at school, and Rasheed's suicide? Do these narratives jar with the light tone of the rest of the novel? Are they convincing?

10. Describe the contribution of the depiction of the world of

music to the portrait of Hindu-Muslim relations in the novel. Seth has said the novel is "in part" a plea for religious tolerance: trace the development of this theme through the narrative, commenting on the contribution of Lata's relationship with Kabir, Maan and Firoz's friendship, the land reform acts, the Raja of Marh's plans to build a temple and the two riots which occur between different religious groups. Is the novel as hopeful about friendship across the two communities as it is pessimistic about the opportunities for communal violence?

11. Seth in *Garavi Gujarat* describes the book as an "Indian novel." To what extent can the Indian setting of the novel be ignored and *A Suitable Boy* be read simply as a love story? Is it only the content of the novel which is Indian or are certain formal features governed by traditions of Indian narrative?

12. Does Seth attempt to represent the whole of India in his novel? What picture of India is painted in *A Suitable Boy*? Do you agree with Pico Iyer and Anita Desai that one of its strengths is its everyday quality, and if so how is this quality produced?

13. Do you agree with Lord Gowrie that the book is in need of a good edit? If so, what should have been cut, if not, what ties the book together? In what ways is the novel's structure governed by its attempts to depict an entire society?

14. What does the Calcutta subplot add to the novel? Is it purely a humorous diversion?

15. Haresh fights and wins a battle at Praha to increase production and levels of pay. What does this tell us about him and about the possibilities for effecting change in India? What other processes of change in society are depicted in the novel?

16. To what extent do you follow the internal politics of the Congress Party? Do you feel that much of the detail is going over your head, or are the complexities clearly represented? What

does this add to the appreciation of India as a democracy? Tolstoy, in *War and Peace*, famously depicted the real historical figure of Napoleon. How does the inclusion of the real historical figure of Nehru affect the fictional world of the novel?

17. Is the land-reform subplot the least integrated part of the novel or do you enjoy the drama of Rasheed's family in Debaria and the passage of the Act through the courts? Are the various strands of this story sufficiently interwoven? Do you take sides in the debate, or are your sympathies equally divided between the exploited peasant and the Nawab Sahib? What does this narrative contribute to the theme of India as a fledgling democracy?

18. Did you enjoy the evocation of the world of Indian classical music? To what extent is it bound up with the traditions of the courtesan? Is Seth in danger here of depicting India as exotic in a way that he was anxious to avoid?

19. Does the cassette version of the novel gain from its tighter structure and does it suggest that a film version of the novel, with all the need for cutting that would have entailed, would have been successful? What does the cassette version gain from being read by the author?

20. Which elements have caused this novel to be considered populist? Are the comparisons to a Mills & Boon novel, or a melodrama, appropriate? Is this a slur on the novel?

21. Do the untranslated words from Hindi and Urdu interrupt the flow of the story? Is it always easy to understand what they mean from their context? Would the book be poorer for their omission? There are many instances of idiosyncratic and non-standard English; to what uses are they put?

22. Are comparisons with George Eliot, Dickens, Tolstoy, Austen, Fielding or Richardson warranted? How far can they be taken?

23. How much does *A Suitable Boy* have in common with other Indian English novels? Do you think there is a school of Indian English Literature? If so, does it divide, in the words of Pico Iyer, into two camps of "pinwheeling invention" and "compassionate realism"? Is the contrast between Seth and Rushdie overstated?

24. Is each work of Seth's completely different from the previous one or do common threads link his novels, poetry, and other writing?

FURTHER READING

Works by Seth

Mappings, Calcutta Writers' Workshop, 1981; Delhi: Penguin, 1994.

From Heaven Lake: Travels Through Sinkiang and Tibet, London: Hogarth Press, 1983.

The Humble Administrator's Garden, Manchester and New York: Carcanet, 1985.

The Golden Gate, London: Faber, 1986.

All You Who Sleep Tonight, London: Faber, 1990.

Three Chinese Poets: Translations of Poems By Wang Wei, Li Bai and Du Fu, London: Faber, 1992.

Beastly Tales From Here and There, London: Phoenix, 1993.

A Suitable Boy, London: Phoenix, 1993.

A Suitable Boy, (4 cassettes) London: Harpercollins, 1994.

A Suitable Boy, (cassette). London: BBC, 2002.

Arion & The Dolphin, London: Phoenix, 1994.

Koi achcha-sa Ladaka, trans. into Hindi by Gopal Gandhi, New Delhi: Vani Prakashan, 1998.

An Equal Music, London: Phoenix, 1999.

Reviews and Interviews

Bal, Sambit. "Finding out about the Suitable Boy"

Bailey, Paul. "Deserting the Ordinary for the Grandiose." *Weekend Telegraph* 20 March 1993, p.xx.

Bookseller, 20 August 1993.

Buchan, James. "A Foreign Country is the Past." *Spectator*, 27 March 1993, p.31.

Catling, Patrick Skene. "Caste in a Modern Light." *Evening Standard*, 18 March 1993, p.45

———— "Books of the Year." *Spectator*, 20 November 1993.

Coles, Joanna. "A Suitable Soap Goes the Literary Distance with 1,400-page tome." *Guardian*, 5 November 1992.

Davis, Dick. "Byron Goes to San Francisco." *Sunday Telegraph*, 29 June 1986.

Desai, Anita. "Sitting Pretty." *New York Review of Books*, 27 May 1993, p.22–26.

Dougary, Ginny. *HQ*. July/August 1993, p.69.

Ellison, Mike. "Choice Words for Booker Judges as Favourite is Left on Shelf." *Guardian*, 23 September 1993, p.26.

Field, Michele. "Vikram Seth." *Publishers Weekly*, 10 May 1993, pp.46–47.

Filkins, Peter. "Seth's *Suitable Boy*: Courtships and Chaos." *USA Today*, 5 July 1993.

Fishlock, Trevor. "All Indian Life and Love is Here." *Sunday Telegraph*, 21 March 1993, p.10.

Gee, Maggie, "Double Helpings of the Food of Love." *Daily Telegraph*, 3 April 1999.

Lord Gowrie. "Literary Critics Brought to Book." Letter to the *Guardian*, 25 September 1993.

Greenstreet, Rosanna. "The Questionnaire:Vikram Seth." *Guardian*, 17 April 1993, p.70.

Garavi Gujarat. "The Astounding Success of Vikram Seth " unsigned 3 April 1993.

Haggar, Nadia. *Omnibus*. BBC, 2 March 1994.

Hajari, Nisid. "Vikram Seth's Genre-Bender." *Village Voice*, 18 May 1993, pp.68–69.

Hitchinson, David. Personal Correspondance with the author, December 2001.

Howard, Philip. "Book Buyers Clear Shelves." *Times*, 23 March 1993

Iyer, Pico. "India Day by Day." *Times Literary Supplement*, 19 March 1993, p.20.

——— "The Empire Writes Back." *Time*, 8 February 1993, No.6.

Jenkyns, Richard. "As the Raj Turns." *New Republic*, 14 June 1993, pp.41–44.

Johnson, Daniel. "Seth's Subcontinent of a Novel." *The Times*, 25 March 1993, p.37.

——— "Words for Music Perhaps." *Daily Telegraph*, 10 April 1999, p.22.

Johnson, Rob. "Potent View of India." 19 June 1933

Jones, Lewis. "The Shock of the Conventional." *Sunday Telegraph*, 28 March 1993: XII.

Kemp, Peter. "A Caste of Thousands." *Sunday Times*, 21 March 1993, p.7.

Khair, Tabish. "Oh Boy." *Sunday Times of India*, 28 February 1993.

Koenig, Rhoda. "Whoa, Boy." *New York*, 17 May 1993, pp.84, 87.

Krishnan, S. "Not a Nostalgic Raj Book." *Indian Review of Books*, 7 March 1993.

Lambert, Angela. "Grey by Name, Passionate by Nature: The Famously Charming Lord Gowrie." *Independent*, 5 October 1993, p.16.

Lanchester, John. "Indian Summa." *London Review of Books*, 22 April 1993, p.9.

McGirk, Tim. "Playing Happy Families in Brahmpur." *Independent*, 27 March 1993, p.31.

Nevin, Charles. "Captain Moonlight: Not on the List." *Independent on Sunday*, 17 October 1993, p.28.

Onslow, James Hughes. "Removing the Stain on President Nixon." *Evening Standard*, 10 June 1994, p.15.

Pass Notes. "No. 114, Vikram Seth." *Guardian*, 22 March 1993.

Patel, Sonai. "Threadbare." *Sunday Free Press*, 7 March 1933

Robinson, Eugene. "A Tolstoy On His First Try." *Washington Post*, 1 May 1993a:G1, G6.

—— "Indian Author's Rendezvous With Fame." *International Herald Tribune*, 5 May 1993b.

Rocco, Fiammetta. "How We Met: Vikram Seth and Giles Gordon." *Independent on Sunday*, 4 April 1993, p.77.

Roy, Amit. "The Most Suitable Boy." *Indian Telegraph*, 29 August 1992.

Seth, Vikram. Advanced Publicity, Phoenix House Publicity Department, 1992.

—— Letter to The *Times*, 26 March 1993.

—— An Equal Music: An Evening with Vikram Seth at The New Ambassadors Theatre, London 17 January 2000.

—— Commemorating R.K. Narayan at The Nehru Centre, London. 11 June 2000.

Teller, Neville. Personal correspondance with the author, November 2001.

Towers, Robert. "Good Enough for her Mother's Mother's Mother." *New York Times*, 9 May 1993, p.3.

Tressider, Maggie. *Sunday Telegraph*, 15 March 1993: Review, 3.

Trivedi, Harish. "Translation as Recovery: *A Suitable Boy* as *Koi Achcha-sa Ladaka*." *The Book Review*, Vol. XXII, Number 9, September 1998, pp.30–31.

Watkins, Susan Alice. "Slowly and Softly Across the Great Gangetic Plain." *Literary Review*, April 1993, p.19–20.

White, Judith. "Saga of Seth." *Sun-Herald*, 4 April 1993, p.101.

Wood, James. "A Suitable Boy." *Guardian*, 16 March 1993, p.9.

—— "Edinburgh Festival: Accidents Will Happen." *Guardian*, 2 September 1993, p.9.

Woodward, Richard, B. "Vikram Seth's Big Book." *New York Times*, 2 May 1993, p.32.

Yardley, Jonathan. "A Dickens For the Subcontinent." *Washington Post*, 25 April 1993, p.3.

Longer Articles and Books

Agarwalla, Shyam. *Vikram Seth's A Suitable Boy; Search for an Indian Identity*. New Delhi: Prestige 1995.

Ashton, Rosemary. Introduction to *Middlemarch*, London: Penguin 1994.

Atkins, Angela. "Land as Legislative Space in Vikram Seth's *A Suitable Boy* and Phanishwarnath Renu's *Maila anchal*." *SOAS Literary Review* (<www2.soas.ac.uk/soaslit>) 2001.

Chaudhuri, Amit (ed.) *The Picador Book of Modern Indian Literature*. London: Picador 2001.

Khilnani, Sunil. *The Idea of India*. London:Penguin 1997.

Lowe, N.J. *The Classical Plot and the Invention of Western Narrative*. Cambridge: Cambridge University Press, 2000.

Morse, Ruth. "Rooted Cosmopolite: Vikram Seth and 'the Scars of *Middle-march*.' " *Etudes Britannique Contemporaines*, No. 5, 1994.

Mukherjee, Meenakshi. *The Twice Born Fiction: Themes and Techniques of the Indian Novel in English*. New Delhi: Heinemann, 1971.

——— *Realism and Reality: The Novel and Society in India*. New Delhi: Oxford University Press, 1985.

Myers, David. "Vikram Seth's Epic Renunciation of the Passions: Deconstructing Moral Codes in *A Suitable Boy*," in *Indian Literature Today*, ed. by R.K. Dharwari. New Delhi, Vol. i, 1994:79–102.

Pandurang, Mala. Vikram Seth: Multiple Locations, Multiple Affiliation. New Delhi: Rawat, 2001.

Rushdie, Salman. *Imaginary Homelands: Essays and Criticism 1981–91*. London: Granta, 1991.

——— and Elizabeth West (eds.) *The Vintage Book of Indian Writing 1947–1997*. London: Vintage, 1997.

Srivastava, Neelam. "The Languages of the Nation in Vikram Seth's *A Suitable Boy*." Unpublished paper, 2000.

——— "The Multi-Lingual Context of Indian Fiction in English." *Anglistica*, 5:1, 2001.

Watt, Ian. *The Rise of the English Novel*. Harmondsworth: Peregrine Books, 1963.

Williams, Raymond. *The Country and the City*. St Albans: Paladin, 1975.

Websites

Book of the Month Club <*www.bomc.com/archives/1993*>

Contemporary Poetry Review <*www.cprw.com/patel/vikram.htm*>

Emory University <*www.emory.edu/English/Bahri/seth.html*>
Doon   School   <*www.doonschool.com*>,   <*www.dsobs.org*>,
<*www.doononline.net/highlights/seth/contemporary.htm*>
Guardian Talk <*http://booktalk.guardian.co.uk*> The Talk, Vikram
Seth online, started by jjordan1 on 26th Feb 2001.
Random   House   <*www.randomhouse.com/boldtype/0599/seth/*
interview.html>
Rediff.com <*www.rediff.com/chat/vikchat.htm*>
Stanford   University   Alumni   <*www.standfordalumni.org/new/*
magazine/1999/mayjun/article/seth.htm>

Works by Other Indian Writers Mentioned

Bisham, Sahni. *Tamas* trans. from Hindi by Jai Ratan. New Delhi: Penguin
     1998.
Kesavan, Mukul. *Looking Through Glass*. London: Vintage, 1996.
Mistry, Rohinston. *A Fine Balance*. London: Faber, 1996.
Narayan, R.K. *Man-Eater of Malguidi*. London: Penguin, 1983 (first pub-
     lished 1961).
——— *Malgudi Days*. London: Penguin, 1984 (first published 1972).
Premchand. *Gift of a Cow* trans. from Hindi by Gordon Roadarmel. Lon-
     don: Allen and Unwin, 1968.
Rao, Raja. *Kanthapura*. Delhi: Oxford University Press, 1996 (first pub-
     lished 1938).
Renu, Phanishwarnath. *The Soiled Border* trans. from Hindi by Indira
     Junghare. New Delhi: Chanakya publications, 1991.
Rushdie, Salman. *Midnight's Children*. London: Jonathan Cape, 1981.
Sealy, I. Allen. *The Everest Hotel*. London: Doubleday, 1998.
Sidhwa, Bapsi. *Ice-Candy-Man*. New Delhi: Penguin, 1989.
Singh, Kushwant. *Train to Pakistan*. New Delhi: Ravi Dayal, 1988 (first
     published 1956).
Tharoor, Shashi *The Great Indian Novel*. London: Viking, 1989.